Why Does This Keep Happening to Me?

The Seven Crises We All Experience and How to Overcome Them

Alan Downs, Ph.D.

A Fireside Book
Published by Simon & Schuster
New York   London   Sydney   Singapore

Fireside

Rockefeller Center
1230 Avenue of the Americas
New York, NY 10020

Fireside and colophon are registered trademarks
of Simon & Schuster, Inc.

All the examples included in this book are real, although the names, locations,
and other identifying characteristics have been changed
to protect the individuals' privacy.

Designed by William Ruoto

Manufactured in the United States of America

1   3   5   7   9   10   8   6   4   2

Library of Congress Cataloging-in-Publication Data

Downs, Alan.
Why does this keep happening to me? : the seven crises we all
experience and
how to overcome them / Alan Downs.
p. cm.
"A Fireside book."
Includes bibliographical references.
1. Self-defeating behavior. 2 Self-defeating behavior—Case studies. I. Title
BF637.S37 D68 2002
158—dc21
2001049634
ISBN 0-7432-0572-3

For information regarding special discounts for bulk
purchases, please contact Simon & Schuster Special Sales at
1-800-456-6798 or business@simonandschuster.com

Acknowledgments

Thanking the friends and colleagues who have contributed to my work is a truly difficult task. I worry as I write these words of gratitude that I will inadvertently leave a name out or somehow fail to express the fullness of my appreciation. Nevertheless, here is my best try.

To my parents, Don and Eunice Downs, to whom I have dedicated this book, I want to express my love and gratitude for everything you've done to make my life full and complete.

To my dearest friends, without you I would never have found the courage to write and to put my work out in the world for all to see. Thank you Claude Harris, Blake Hunter, Dale Monteith, Nesha Morse, Frank Pontes, Annette Simmons, Kevin Sloan, Phil Tecau, Bob Ward, and Ron Williams.

To my sister and fellow therapist, Donna McCoy, thank you for showing me and all your clients what courage and forgiveness really mean.

To my wonderful literary agent, Susan Schulman, thank you for always being there with the perfect word of encouragement and expert business advice.

Acknowledgments

To my editor, Nicole Diamond, thank you for believing in my work and for being patient enough to craft it into this book.

To my Santa Fe friends, Peter Mattair, David Naylor, and Betsy Peterson, thank you.

Finally, to Steve Sugarman—without your support this book would have never happened. Thank you for all that you do.

[To Mom and Dad—Thank you]

Contents

Contents

Introduction

Not all that long ago, my life fell completely apart. The relationship I had cherished for ten years and thought would last a lifetime fell to pieces. My practice slowed dramatically, and I had little motivation to do anything about it. I was tired and confused. Every time I tried to improve my life, it seemed to only get worse. I lost interest in my work, my relationships all seemed to end in disaster, and I was living thousands of miles away from my family.

"For God's sake," I'd tell myself, "you're a psychologist! You know how to break out of this funk." I'd helped clients make it through these kinds of dark crises and had even helped a few colleagues do the same, but I was embarrassed that it was happening to me now. *And it was happening to me.* I couldn't help myself. My life was spinning out of control. No matter what I did, nothing seemed to change for the better. What I thought was the worst of it only seemed to give way to something even more painful. I now deeply understood the desperation that continues to drive so many clients into therapists' offices. I kept asking myself, "What's wrong with me? Why can't I pull out of this?"

You won't understand what I'm talking about until you go through it, and at some point in your life you will go through it. Chances are that if you've picked up this book you know exactly what I'm talking about. No matter what you do, your life doesn't seem to improve. Your life has become something to struggle through, rather than live—much less enjoy. This book is for you.

It will get better if you will take this book seriously. What I share with you in this book isn't some theoretical doctrine or psychobabble. It's practical advice that I learned the hard way. I discovered it because *I had to*. If you're going through a crisis now, you know exactly what I mean. Things can't keep getting worse. What's the point of living that kind of life?

There is help. You can survive your crisis. You can get back on track. You can regain control of your life.

When the Story Keeps Repeating

"Why do I keep marrying men who turn out to be jerks?"

"Why do I keep losing and then gaining weight?"

"Why do I always end up working for a creep?"

"Why can't I ever seem to get ahead financially?"

"Why am I always fighting with my kids?"

"Why am I disappointed with my life more often than not?"

"Why can't I seem to break free from this awful rut?"

Do you find yourself worried about why your life seems to be going in circles, rather than moving forward? Are you sometimes a little panicked by the prospect that you may never end this seemingly unending chain of repeating circumstances?

This time, it wasn't supposed to happen. This time, things were going to turn out better. You thought you had learned your lesson, but somehow you've landed in the very same painful place.

How many times have you said this? This time I won't marry someone who turns out to be a jerk like the one before. Or maybe, this time I'll make sure the boss isn't a tyrant before I take the job. This time, I won't get myself so far into debt.

And then, despite your very best effort, you find yourself right back where you were before. The new relationship is just like the last one, the new boss is even worse than the one you quit or the bank account is overdrawn, *again*. What's going wrong? What keeps you from breaking free from those old painful patterns? Why can't you seem to take control of your life and change it for the better?

You're not alone. Therapists' offices around the world are flooded with people frustrated that their lives keep repeating the same painful scenarios. They have tried and tried, but they keep hitting a brick wall and can't seem to break free of an old, painful pattern. They are asking the same question you are: "Why does this keep happening to me?"

This book will help you find the answer to that question, and more important, help you find a way to break the bonds that have held you in the same painful patterns. It isn't magic, or a quick fix, but rather it is solid advice that I've accumulated over years of working with people just like you. In fact, what this book offers is something that everyone who finds peace and fulfillment in life has discovered—I've simply tried to put it down in words that might help you to find it more easily.

You're not sick, broken, mentally ill, or inadequate. You

don't lack will power. You aren't cursed with a life of misery. What you are experiencing now is something that *everyone* experiences. How you handle this situation will determine if you break free or stay stuck in the same self-defeating cycle. This book is here to guide you through the pain to a better, more fulfilling life.

"So, if nothing is wrong with me, why do I feel so terrible?" Good question—and let's get started answering it. First, what you're going through has a name: *crisis.*

A crisis isn't life-threatening, but it is painful, and if it continues, it can be debilitating. When you're in the middle of it, there's no place more miserable.

A crisis happens when you experience a painful void in your life. You've done everything you know, and still, you wind up at the same place, with the same results you swore you wouldn't repeat again. So here you are, right back where you never wanted to be.

Everyone experiences crises. High-ranking executives, ministers, therapists, and Pulitzer Prize–winning authors all have crises. Smart people, rich people, happily married people, single people, old people, young people all experience crisis. It's easy to think that smart or successful people have no crises in their lives, but that is dead wrong. Money, intelligence, power, and success are no insurance against crisis, and in fact, often make crises worse. *Everyone* experiences them.

There are four ways in which crises can manifest in your life. They can be latent crises, inflamed crises, suppressed crises, or resolved crises. To begin with, a crisis first appears in your life as a latent crisis. That is, it is present but is not causing you any pain. For example, you may be aware that spirituality is important, but feel no urgent need to find spiritual answers for your life. In this case, your spiritual crisis is a latent crisis.

If, however, your husband dies suddenly and unexpectedly, you may find yourself in urgent need of spiritual answers about the fundamental meaning of life and eternity. Suddenly, your latent crisis has become inflamed. You're in pain and needing some solid answers. An inflamed crisis is the most painful and most distressing form of crisis.

What makes a latent crisis become an inflamed crisis? Almost always it is a painful or traumatic event that activates the latent crisis and starts causing you pain. You lose your job. Your relationship falls apart. You have a heart attack and suddenly must scale back your activities. Your son fails in school. Your best friend no longer wants to see you.

Whatever the event might be, it unleashes the energy of the latent crisis, and you begin to experience great distress. It's more than just the pain of a broken relationship or a lost job— you begin to have some serious and painful questions about your life. The questions keep you up at night and hound you during the day. There's no escape from a crisis that has become inflamed.

The point at which you experience a crisis is when it becomes inflamed. When the crisis is latent, you don't experience it as a crisis—in fact, you may not be aware of it at all. It takes a triggering event to bring a latent crisis into your full awareness and make it inflamed.

Once it is inflamed, you have two choices: You can either suppress the crisis (for example, by immediately dating your high-school boyfriend after your divorce and then marrying him three months later) or you can take steps to resolve your crisis—a process that you'll learn about in this book.

When you're locked into a repeating pattern that you just can't seem to break, it happens for one reason: You're suppressing a crisis rather than resolving it. A suppressed crisis occurs when you experience a crisis and rather than confront and resolve it, you push it back into the recesses of your mind in an effort to avoid the pain it is causing you. There are many ways you might suppress a crisis. For example, you might distract yourself with busyness, or occupy yourself with addiction, or throw yourself into a mind-numbing depression.

However you do it, suppressing a crisis has one monumental negative side effect: *It keeps you stuck in the same repeating circumstances.* Because you're coming from a place of fear and avoidance, you don't move forward, and instead remain in the same painful situations. Suppressing a crisis takes lots of energy. It slowly depletes your psychic resources, leaving you unable to grow, take risks, and move forward.

There are seven basic crises that you will experience in your life. Every single person will experience these seven crises, regardless of race, education, or background. Chances are, you're experiencing one of them right now. How you respond to these crises, whether you suppress them or confront them, will dictate whether you are able to move on with your life. If you're stuck repeating the same painful patterns over and over again, it is because one of these seven crises is in your life and you are not confronting it. This book will help you identify the unresolved crisis you are suppressing and will teach you how to confront and resolve it. A little further in the book there will be a quiz that will help you to identify your crisis and will direct you to a specific chapter that will help you resolve it.

So what are the seven basic crises that everyone experiences? They are, in no particular order:

- The Crisis of Passion
- The Crisis of Contact
- The Crisis of Self-Confidence
- The Crisis of Individuation
- The Crisis of Fear
- The Crisis of Spiritual Meaning
- The Crisis of Broken Dreams

Some people immediately suppress a crisis as soon as it becomes inflamed, living rigid lives that are dedicated to avoiding the crises that lurk just beneath the surface of their carefully crafted exteriors. Others live in a state of continuously inflamed crisis, unable to suppress it and reluctant to take on the task of resolving it. Still others experience each crisis as it occurs and then go about the work of finding healthy resolution. The goal of this book is to help you learn this process and to resolve each crisis as you experience it.

Let me tell you how some of my clients have experienced crisis:

MARIANNE'S CRISIS

When she walked into my office, the frustration she was feeling oozed from her. The way she walked with leaden feet, the half-hearted smile, and the downward gaze—they all betrayed her heart. And it said volumes more than she could have told me in ten therapy sessions. She was overwhelmed with frustration.

At first glance, Marianne appeared to be a successful woman. She was attractive and dressed smartly. With her slim briefcase clutched in one hand and the other ready to be extended and pull you into her world with a firm handshake, there was no doubt that Marianne meant business. As I later learned, Marianne had a very successful career.

But the day she came to see me, business success wasn't the problem. She was thirty-five years old and never married, although she had been briefly engaged during college. She didn't feel the need for a traditional relationship and she liked the independence offered by not having a husband waiting at home for her.

What was deeply troubling Marianne was a realization that had hit her just a few days earlier. She seemed to be incapable of having a relationship with anyone other than a married man, and those relationships always seemed to follow the same course—passionate meetings, promises of divorce that never happened, and eventually her breaking off the relationship in frustration. Over and over this same pattern had repeated itself.

The weight of this crisis was wearing on her trademark confidence and enthusiasm. She found herself sleeping late, missing deadlines, and unable to do anything other than the most routine tasks. It wasn't as if she was depressed, she said, it was more like sleepwalking. She was going through the motions, but not feeling a thing.

"What is so terribly wrong with me?" she begged. "Why can't I have a long-term loving and committed relationship with a *single* man?"

By the end of our first hour together, she was telling me that maybe she "just wasn't cut out" to have a relationship. She was, after all, very successful, and in her mind, that was quite an accomplishment for a woman working in a business that was dominated by "the good old boys." Maybe that would just have to be enough.

Marianne was caught in a crisis. It wasn't a relationship crisis—it was a crisis deep within Marianne. For years she had denied that the crisis existed, and she continued to repeat the same dead-end relationships. Now, suddenly, the pent-up pain of all those years in denial rushed forward and overwhelmed her. It seemed no matter what she did, it made no difference. At the end of the day, it was always the same: Her lover went back to his wife and she was once again alone and very much on her own.

MID-CAREER COLLAPSE

A few years ago I worked with an executive named Don who was, in the mind of his company's human resources director, in a career death spiral. After a string of bad quarterly results and failed programs, this previously successful executive had become withdrawn and had "lost his edge." By the time I was called, Don was on the verge of being fired.

Don described his situation to me as a midlife crisis. He had realized over the past few years that he hated his job (even though he did it quite well) and wasn't sure if he wanted to be married anymore. Every week or so, he would take a business trip and extend it for a night or two in Las Vegas, where he would secretly spend the days and nights like the big-spending bachelor he wished he were.

Throughout this time, Don had become increasingly depressed and gave very little energy to his work. At first, he was able to coast on his past successes, but after a few years of this, his negligence really started to show and his boss threatened that if he didn't improve, he might lose his job.

Don was thoroughly convinced that his problem was being too "tied down," and the only escape he could envision was a divorce and a career change. As we worked together, it became clear that Don's love for his wife hadn't really diminished; it was that Don's whole world had become colored with his resentment. It was resentment that he had somehow not become what he wanted, and yet, he didn't quite know what that was. He just knew that there wasn't any passion in his life. He was full of blame for everything around him—his job, the company, his parents, and his wife.

One day, quite unexpectedly for Don, his wife moved out of the house and asked for a divorce. You would think this turn of events would have solved Don's problem of being "too tied down," but it didn't. In fact, it threw Don into a state of depression that ultimately caused him to lose his job and most of his friends. Now, he was alone, single, and truly miserable.

JEANNIE'S BROKE AGAIN

Jeannie was energetic and full of ideas. She had a brilliant imagination and loved to travel. So it made perfect sense to her that after a painful bankruptcy and divorce, owning her own dress shop would be the perfect career for her. The shop would give her the opportunity to buy all kinds of interesting clothes and display them creatively for her customers. She could travel to the Orient and Europe once a year to bring back all the treasures she could find to sell in her shop.

So she borrowed every nickel she could from everyone she dared ask and opened her shop. She filled the shop with everything she could afford to buy—all the kinds of clothes she would want to wear. Carefully, she displayed her clothing, trying hard to keep her shop from looking like the women's department in one of those slick and impersonal department stores.

After a year of scraping to pay the shop rent, Jeannie had to close down. It seemed that her customers, the few that she had, didn't really share her taste in clothing. They would occasionally stop in and peruse the displays and maybe buy a small handbag or scarf, but rarely anything of much value.

Sitting on my couch, Jeannie was frustrated and depressed. She had followed her passion, and wasn't that supposed to "make the money come"? Now, she was right back where she started, only worse. Not only was she bankrupt again, she had lost some of her closest friends, who had loaned her money to open the shop and keep it going. One by one, they had all distanced themselves from her as her requests for money had become more frequent.

Jeannie felt like a total failure. She was weighted down with a heavy guilt over losing so much of her friends' money. She described herself as a loser. Maybe she just wasn't smart enough to make a decent living.

The truth was, Jeannie wasn't a loser. She was caught between her passion and earning a living. It seemed that every time she allowed herself to follow her heart, she wound up broke again. Should she build her life on making a respectable living or follow her passion?

In time, Jeannie would understand and embrace another option that she just couldn't see at the time. She discovered she wasn't doomed to bounce between her heart and her head, or her wallet and her talent. What Jeannie needed, and finally achieved, was a breakthrough from the crisis she was facing.

STUCK . . . AS IT HAPPENS AGAIN

Marianne, Don, and Jeannie were all caught in painful stories that kept repeating. It was as if they were running but not going anywhere, or trying to scream for help but not making a sound. Their worlds, once full of opportunity and challenge, became obstacle courses full of danger and drudgery. They each reached a dead end in life—a place where it seemed as if they had no choice but to remain in misery. They tried to make things better by suppressing their crises, but despite their struggles, the crises only got worse.

In time, they were able to find the answers they needed to resolve their crises and put their lives back on track. What may surprise you as we look at their journeys (and the journeys of many others) is that the real solution to their problems wasn't what they first imagined. There was something deeper going on within Marianne, Don, and all others caught spinning their psychic wheels. It was far more than the armchair diagnoses of "poor relationship skills" or "midlife crisis." They were caught in the ironclad grip of unresolved and suppressed crisis.

It's a place where most of us find ourselves at some point, and it can be both lonely and intensely frustrating. But there is help. There is a way out of the trap that seems to have caught you. You must first confront the crisis and dig to the core to discover what is causing it. In this book, I will show you how to identify your crisis, confront it, and get the breakthrough you are seeking.

How have you felt alone, different, flawed, or inadequate as a result of experiencing a crisis?

BUT WHY *CRISIS?*

At this point you may be asking, why must there be *crisis?* Can't I just get insight and apply it to my life without having a *crisis?* That's a good question, and frankly, it's at the core of why so much of the self-help movement has failed. There are many thousands of books and seminars promising a shortcut through all the difficulties of creating a fulfilling life. By now, most of us have tried those shortcuts, and we know they just don't work for the long haul.

All the fairy tales about life (including a whole truckload of get-well-quick books and tapes) say that life can be painless and deliriously happy all the time. Okay, stop and think about this for a minute. How many people do you know well who are *deliriously happy all the time?* As a therapist and author, I know a lot of people, and I don't know one who fits into this category. I'll bet you don't either.

You *will* be unhappy from time to time, you *will* experience some pain, and you *will not* escape this life without your share of difficulty. What you don't have to experience is constant, repeating misery. You can feel an abiding sense of satisfaction and fulfillment throughout your life. Most important, you are not doomed to a life of repeating frustration and sadness.

Now, let me return to the question of "Why crisis?": Yes, there must be *crisis.* Yes, there must be a certain amount of confusion and psychological pain. *If there were no confusion and pain there would be no real learning.* This is probably the most important insight toward changing your life for the better: From time to time, crisis *will* come. Once you make peace with this, you stop fighting the process and allow it to begin to shape your life for your highest good.

When tragedy strikes, the first natural response is "Why me?" To which the world callously responds "Why not you?" Painful circumstances are part of every life—no one leaves this planet unscathed. The amount of psychological pain you experience in life is not determined by what happens to you, but by how you handle your life's crises. If you suppress those crises, you will live much of your life in psychological misery. If, on the other hand, you learn to face your crises and deal with them squarely, you will be free to create the life you want.

Where does this process of crisis and resolution come from? I believe it is the way that nature helps us along our journey. After years of working with people in pain from all walks of life, I am convinced that everything happens in our lives for a reason—*a good reason*. Each crisis has a very important lesson to teach us.

Maybe you're more comfortable thinking about this in practical terms. Think about pain as your biological teacher. Remember when you were a child and put your hand on a hot stove? What happened? You felt pain and the pain prompted you to action. More important, the pain also embedded an important lesson in your mind about not touching objects that are hot. That's why nature uses pain—to teach us important lessons. Your body feels pain when something is wrong and needs to be changed. Pain is a very helpful biological process. So it is with your state of mind—you feel psychological pain when you need to change.

By clinging to the idea that you should be happy all the time, and that if you're not, something must be desperately wrong with you, you are preventing yourself from experiencing the very happiness you deserve in life. In fact, there's no surer way to misery. If you try, as many do, to be happy all the time, you will never allow yourself to deal honestly with the crises that occur in your life. Instead, you will spend much of your time hiding the crisis pain behind a suffocating smiley-face façade.

Happiness is something we all strive for, and at the same time, we can never have a steady diet of it. *Being happy is entirely dependent upon your willingness to forsake the pursuit of happiness and face the difficult truths about yourself.* To be sure, you can have a great deal of happiness in this life, but finding it means resolving each crisis as it occurs.

The pain you feel in crisis is a signal for you to learn and grow. When you heed that signal and subsequently resolve the crisis, you find yourself happier and more fulfilled. On the other hand, if the crisis remains unresolved, the pain begins to compound and undermine your confidence. It's a double whammy—the longer the crisis continues, the worse it gets.

Take Marianne, for example. Her predicament is like that of many others who live in a state of unresolved crisis. Not only were her relationship choices not working, *she kept making the same choices.* Marianne was bright, energetic, and by all accounts, a very likable woman. Simply telling her to make a different choice would not have solved her problems—she already knew that she wanted something different. Having lived in unresolved crisis for so long, she now felt incapable of making different choices. She saw herself make the same mistake so many times that she no longer had the courage to make a different choice.

> *How has the idea that you must be happy all the time or something is wrong with you affected your life? How have you tried to escape the normal pain of living?*

IS THIS YOUR LIFE?

Let me show you just how important crises are to creating a fulfilling life. Imagine this . . .

You walk into a dimmed theater, and as your eyes adjust to the dark, you find a seat and settle in. The theater is packed with people and the movie is scheduled to begin at any moment. The curtain parts and the previews of coming attractions begin. One of them catches your eye and you make a mental note to see that one when it is released. The curtain closes and reopens as the feature film begins.

The music swells and a hush falls over the crowd as the title appears on the screen. As you watch the opening scenes, it all seems vaguely familiar to you. Perhaps you have seen this movie before? No, that couldn't be—it's a new release. The characters you definitely know very well, but how?

Then it dawns on you—this is the story of your life. You're that kid on the screen, and those are your parents and your brothers and sisters. You start to feel uneasy and wonder, do all these people know that this is your life? Then a horrible pang hits you in the pit of your stomach—surely it won't show *everything!*

Just imagine for a moment that this is really happening to you. If you're like most people, you will be riveted by the movie and watching every moment. It's all about you, and it's bigger than life up on the screen. And when the movie ends, it stops right where you are, sitting in the movie theater.

Take some time now and imagine the movie of your life. In your mind's eye, watch the screen and all the events that have followed through your life. Begin as early as you can remember and slowly bring yourself through the teenage years, early adult and adult years to the present day . . .

Now think of yourself as a movie reviewer for a respected publication. What would you have to say about this movie? Did it start off with promise, but fizzle out during the last half? Is it monotonous, repeating the same situations over and over again? Is it filled with stock characters, having the same relationships over and over again? Is it a soap opera–like drama that goes from one scene of betrayal and conflict to another?

Movies are stories, and stories are tales about life. We instinctively recognize a good story. Remember when you were a kid and your parents read you stories before bed? Nobody had to tell you which stories were good stories—you *knew* what a good story was without anyone telling you. Why? Because you were born with an innate sense about what a good, fulfilling, adventurous life is all about. The best stories— the ones you love to read and to watch on the big screen—are only representations of what you know to be true about a fulfilling life.

So how interesting is the movie of your life? Does it seem to drag? Does it get bogged down in the same repeating circumstances? Do you find there is something lacking in the story line?

What makes a really good and satisfying story is a *plot twist*. A plot twist occurs when the action in the story suddenly shifts, and the story heads in a new direction. It's what makes a story interesting—and in large part is the backbone of truly great stories.

If you find that the story of your life is less than fulfilling, there's a good chance that you are avoiding a plot twist. In order to create a plot twist in your life, the action in your life must come to a screeching halt and you must take a step in a different direction. Plot twists utterly change your life—they change *you*. It can seem like pretty scary stuff.

Crisis is the natural cue for a plot twist. Crisis tells you that it's time to change the action and head in a new direction. When you fail to confront a crisis and resolve it, your life doesn't change and the story gets mired in the same repeating circumstances.

Plot twists are never easy. Think about it. Imagine what Scarlett O'Hara must have felt when she made the decision to flee Atlanta and return to Tara. She was utterly terrified—and she did have other options. She could have stayed right where she was. She could have fled north. At that point, there were no guarantees that by returning to Tara she would become anything more than a poor Southern farmer.

Remember the story of the Israelites in slavery in Egypt (portrayed on the big screen in *The Prince of Egypt*)? That story is filled with terrifying plot twists. What if Moses had refused to return from his quiet life in the desert as a shepherd? What if the Israelite slaves had refused to follow this impassioned and somewhat idealistic leader out of Egypt? *War and Peace, Catcher in the Rye, The Great Gatsby,* or *A Tale of Two Cities* wouldn't have been very good stories either if the main characters hadn't experienced at least a few plot twists.

To a certain extent, a plot twist is a step of blind faith. It is a departure from what you've known into new territory and new experiences. When your life's story teeters at the brink of a plot twist, but never takes the turn, it becomes tedious, boring, and very unsatisfying. Who wants to live that story?

When you are faced with crisis, you are faced with the choice to create a plot twist. Crisis is the point where your life story is begging to take a turn. When you deny that crisis and refuse to change the plot, you become stuck in the same old story—repeating it again and again. If you stay there long enough you will begin to lose interest in almost everything—including yourself.

> *How has your life's story been yearning*
> *for a plot twist?*

IT MAKES YOU FEEL HELPLESS

When you continue to suppress a crisis in your life and it lingers unresolved, it begins to destroy your self-esteem and diminish your ability to find resolution. You descend into a state of mind that psychologists call *helplessness.*

One of the most vivid examples of helplessness was an experiment conducted by the now-famous psychologist Martin Seligman. In his early years as a behavioral researcher, Dr. Seligman worked with dogs, trying to identify simpler forms of behavior that might lend some insight into the more complex actions of humans. What the young Dr. Seligman stumbled upon was enlightening.

The experiment Dr. Seligman performed (there were many different variations, so I simply describe the general paradigm) was to put a dog in a box with two compartments. Both compartments were wired to alternately give a mild electrical shock (psychologists have long been fascinated with shocking innocent animals—but that's another story). When one compartment gave a shock, the dog could jump to the other compartment to escape the shock. Quickly, the dogs learned to anticipate the shocks before they happened and would jump to the other side to avoid the pain of being shocked altogether. Soon it became something of a game for the dogs, as they jumped back and forth.

When the dogs were later placed in a box and not allowed to escape the shock, they would at first struggle, claw, and bark trying to exit, but eventually, with repeated shocks, they would stop struggling and would submit to the pain. Many of these dogs went on to develop highly neurotic and maladaptive behavior, such as spinning and incessant tail-biting.

And here's the interesting part of the experiment: Dr. Seligman then put these dogs back into the first box that allowed them to escape when shocked. Guess what? The dogs wouldn't even try to escape. Instead, they cowered in pain as the shocks were administered, just as they had done in the box that had no escape.

What Dr. Seligman illustrated in rather dramatic (if not torturous) style was that when a dog's best efforts are ineffective in avoiding pain, the dog gives up and stops trying. The dog literally becomes helpless.

So it is with you and me. The longer we remain frustrated and in pain, the less likely we are to confront the crisis we are experiencing. We become conditioned to the pain, and while we don't enjoy it, we become accustomed to living with the frustration and misery. In essence, we stop trying.

Like Seligman's dogs, you, too, have developed ways of handling your continued frustration. Perhaps you've experienced depression, defensiveness, emotional hypersensitivity, or uncontrollable anger over the repeating pain in your life. These are all ways in which you express your frustration and sense of helplessness. Nothing you do seems to make a difference, so the frustration builds until it explodes in your life through these natural "pressure valves."

Are there painful areas in your life where you have just given up? How do you express your frustration with those areas?

You don't want to feel helpless, and you don't have to. The first step toward healing is to recognize that at the root of these feelings of helplessness is a suppressed crisis. So let's turn our attention to the process of suppression, and more important, how you can stop doing it.

Won't It Eventually Just Go Away?

[Unnatural Agreements We Keep]

You ask: "Isn't a crisis something that hurts for a while, but if I can endure it, it will eventually go away on its own?"

And your friends tell you: "It's just a phase." "Time heals everything." "You'll get through this—just hang in there."

Crises don't just go away. If you try to ignore them long enough, you'll find a way of suppressing the pain, and the crisis will stay unresolved. You'll start to feel better—until something else triggers it, like when your child talks back to you and you react abusively. Or when your spouse tries to compliment you and all you can hear is an insult. Or when your boss corrects your spelling and you fall to pieces. No, crises don't just go away. They burn inside you until you finally resolve them.

There is a powerful force inside you that will keep you from confronting a crisis when it occurs. This force is called your *agreements*.

Your agreements—the psychological contracts you make with yourself and with other people—determine a surprising amount of your behavior. In fact, the process of day-to-day life is very much about making agreements and working to keep them. Some agreements you make consciously with other people. Other agreements—and these are of primary concern—you make unconsciously, and they govern your behavior in some powerful ways.

What drives you to suppress a crisis is often an unconscious agreement that you are unwilling to break. Instead of experiencing a crisis that you fear may cause you to challenge your agreements, you suppress the crisis with the hope that it will subside and eventually go away.

As you've seen, once a crisis enters into awareness and becomes inflamed, it doesn't go away. No amount of denial or avoidance will resolve it. Instead, it sits on the back burner of your mind, growing more toxic as time goes by. The only thing that suppressing the crisis does is reduce the pain for a time. Before long, the crisis comes roaring back and you must divert your effort to suppressing it again.

The agreements that keep you from resolving your life's crises are *unnatural agreements*. Not only do these agreements hold you back, they must be changed before you can free yourself from the painful patterns you've found yourself stuck in.

Here are a few unnatural agreements that my clients have struggled with . . .

DOROTHY'S DILEMMA

Dorothy came to see me not for herself, she said, but for her son, Tom. Tom, it seems, had always been a good son. He was popular as a child, earned good grades in high school and college, and now held a respected job on Wall Street. There was only one thing about Tom that was out of the ordinary: Tom was gay. Dorothy said that even though she didn't care for it, she had come to terms with his "turning gay" and had learned to live with it.

Recently, it seemed as if Tom had grown distant. He lived in another state and his once-regular visits had become increasingly less frequent. His weekly phone calls had become monthly, and he rarely revealed much about his life to his mother.

Just before seeing me, Dorothy found out, quite by accident, that Tom had been living with another man for almost two years. She was shocked and hurt that he hadn't revealed this to her, but at the same time she didn't want to meet his partner.

During Tom's next visit with his mother, they both came to my office. During our session, we began to uncover some of the unconscious and mostly unspoken agreements between Tom and his mother. Whenever Tom had called his mother and spoken about the men he had been dating, his mother quickly changed the subject. In fact, after he first told her he was gay, they never really discussed the issue—or Tom's romantic interests—again. Now that Tom had met someone whom he loved dearly and who was very much a part of his life, his conversations with his mother had become very superficial and almost meaningless.

The agreement that Tom and Dorothy held between themselves went something like this: "If you *must* be gay, the least you can do is not talk about it." For years, both Tom and Dorothy had clung to this agreement, both honoring their side of it.

Over time, this unconscious agreement had virtually destroyed their relationship. Dorothy had grown into her retirement years and Tom had created a full and loving life for himself and neither one of them really knew about the other. Their agreement had forced them to grow very far apart.

CAROLINE GOES TO WORK

Caroline just knew she had chronic fatigue syndrome, or something like that. She was totally exhausted all the time, but her physician couldn't find anything wrong with her. She'd been checked for just about everything, Epstein-Barr Syndrome, fibromyalgia syndrome, anemia, chronic fatigue syndrome, you name it, they'd tested her for it. She had a perfect bill of health, yet she could hardly drag herself out of bed in the morning.

Caroline was a magazine editor, a job she took after her children went to school. Her husband never saw the need for Caroline to work, since he made plenty of money, and he strongly encouraged her to stay at home. But Caroline loved working and felt she needed to contribute something outside the home, so she continued with her job.

During the course of therapy with Caroline and her husband, they discovered a very important unconscious agreement they had both been keeping. It was: "In exchange for my being able to work outside the home, I'll make sure that *nothing* at home suffers." Caroline had kept this agreement religiously. Every night after work, she rushed home to prepare a big dinner, wash the laundry, clean the house, and tend to the kids. Whenever the children had outside activities, she arranged to escape the office and be there for them.

All told, Caroline's agreement forced her to become a sort of superwoman—doing everything to perfection. She was determined not to fail at work or at home, and it completely exhausted her.

Once Caroline and her husband acknowledged their unconscious agreement and the heavy burden it placed on Caroline, her husband began to take on more responsibility for the household work and her exhaustion began to ease. Looking back, Caroline sees clearly how her unconscious agreement with her husband had driven her to the verge of physical collapse.

CHEAPER BY THE DOZEN

Dale's mother had been dead for ten years when I first met him, but you would never have known that by the way he talked about her. She and Dale had been very close and he had always been "the good son" out of a family of four children. While his siblings were floundering through broken careers and divorces, Dale had a good job and a quiet family. Dale lived with his family less than a mile from his mother's home.

Dale came to see me because his marriage was in trouble. According to him, his wife had become irresponsible with the household budget, and whenever he pointed this out, she became explosively angry with him. He couldn't understand what had brought on this seemingly sudden change.

When I met with Dale's wife, she recounted to me much as Dale had how he had been very close to his mother. His mother had been very frugal—a child of the Great Depression—and never bought anything unless it was on sale. She would travel great distances to visit flea markets and clearance centers to get the best deal. And when she found a great deal, no matter if it was Pepto-Bismol or toothbrushes, she would buy them by the dozens (when she died she had an entire garage and storage locker filled with cases of household products). Wasting money was the cardinal sin for Dale's mother, and she tried to instill this same rigid frugality in her children.

As an adult, even after his mother's death, Dale enforced the same kind of penny-pinching on his family. They were never to shop at the mall or buy anything stylish, because if it were trendy, they were probably paying far too much for it. Over the years Dale's thriftiness had paid off handsomely. At age forty-five he had amassed enough savings to retire if he chose. But the savings were never enough to satisfy Dale, and even though they could live quite comfortably and still have plenty in the bank, he continued to impose his spending limits on himself and his wife.

Now, all the frugality seemed pointless to Dale's wife. "What are we going to do with all that money? When will we ever get to enjoy it?" Her resentment at Dale's "stinginess" had begun to eat away at their relationship.

In working with Dale and his wife, an unconscious agreement between Dale and his deceased mother began to emerge. It was something like: "To be poor is unbearably painful and you must do everything possible to never be poor. You make me proud when you save your money." Dale had spent much of his adult life keeping his side of this bargain. In exchange for his mother's approval, he saved like a miser. In time, Dale was able to examine this agreement and slowly revise it. As he realized that saving money was about earning his mother's love, he was able to relax his strictest spending limits and allow himself and his wife to enjoy some of the money they had both worked so hard to earn.

Can you think of an agreement, spoken or unspoken, that you have made with someone you love? How has it been helpful in the relationship? How has it held you back?

For now, it isn't important to understand the specific crises that Tom, Dorothy, Caroline, and Dale were suppressing. What you need to see is how their agreements worked in the background to hold them back. As long as they lived by these agreements, they weren't free to confront the crises at hand.

The healthiest agreements are conscious (meaning you are aware of them) and are open to revision. When you cling to old agreements that have outlived their usefulness, you bind yourself to the person you used to be but are no longer. Let me put it another way: It is as if you tie yourself tightly with a rope to prevent your own growth. Don't change! Don't learn! Because if you do, you may discover that certain agreements you once made are no longer helping you to be happy and fulfilled.

With whom have you made agreements? Your agreements can be with your parents, your spouse, your siblings, your boss, your friends, and your High Power (God, Nature, The Universe, and so forth). You might be surprised to realize how many agreements you are unconsciously keeping with people and circumstances that have long since passed out of your life. As long as those agreements remain unconscious, you keep them blindly without examining why you keep them.

When I begin to probe the agreements of a group in therapy, and we move past all the surface, easy agreements (for example, "I agree not to criticize my boss and he agrees to keep me employed") to the emotionally charged agreements (for example, "I agreed with my mother that I would *never* turn out to be the failure my father was"), the tears begin to flow and hands start to tremble. For many of us, a great deal of our life has been dictated by unconscious agreements that we made many years ago, perhaps even in childhood. And like good children, we are still striving as adults to keep those old agreements. I can tell you from personal experience that the entry of those agreements into your conscious awareness is at once revealing and deeply moving.

Let me ask the question again: *What agreements are guiding your life?* To help you answer this question, complete the worksheet on pages 44–45. I encourage you to work on this for a while. Think about it in all the places you go each day: in the car, at work, while you exercise, and at home. You'll be surprised at what you learn about yourself.

After you've completed the worksheet and had a chance to examine some of the agreements that have influenced your life, the big question is, "What can you do to change them?"

In some cases, it's simply enough to bring the agreement to conscious awareness. By doing so, you give yourself the opportunity to examine why you keep it and begin to make other choices. The next time you start to act "automatically" on that agreement, you can choose to act another way, knowing that it is the old agreement that is making you feel uncomfortable about change.

In other cases, the agreement is far too ingrained in your life and will require some action on your part before it begins to relinquish control over your life. In these cases, it is critical that you talk with the person with whom you have the agreement. If this person is still living and accessible, then you must spend some

SIGNIFICANT PERSON IN YOUR LIFE	CONSCIOUS AGREEMENTS	UNCONSCIOUS/UNSPOKEN AGREEMENTS
Mother	As long as I am the child you want, you will love me.	We won't talk about my husband (whom you disapprove of).
Father	You will take care of me and provide help if I need it.	I won't confront you about your drinking problem.
Siblings	We won't talk about how you're raising your children.	I will always rescue you when you get into trouble.
Spouse	We will never disagree in public.	I'll ignore your sexual affairs with other women as long as you won't leave me.
Higher Power (God, Nature, The Universe, Luck, etc.)	I will attend church and raise my family to believe in God.	As long as I pray, you won't allow bad things to happen to me or to my family.
Friends	I'll have lunch with you every couple of weeks.	I'll be friends with you as long as you don't ask too much of me.
Yourself	I will postpone my dream until after the kids are grown and out of the house.	I'll stay in this relationship as long as my partner doesn't make me talk about my deepest feelings.

SIGNIFICANT PERSON IN YOUR LIFE	CONSCIOUS AGREEMENTS	UNCONSCIOUS/UNSPOKEN AGREEMENTS	
Mother			
Father			
Siblings			
Spouse			
Higher Power (God, Nature, The Universe, Luck, etc.)			
Friends			
Yourself			

AGREEMENT WORKSHEET

time with him or her discussing your agreement. The person may or may not be willing to acknowledge that this agreement exists, but it doesn't matter—you need to have the conversation. By talking about it with the person with whom the agreement originated, you can break the bonds it holds over you.

Remember the case of Tom and Dorothy? When we first uncovered their agreement not to talk about Tom being gay, Dorothy adamantly denied having any such agreement and was indignant that Tom would suggest she had anything to do with their relationship disintegrating. Remarkably, Tom gently held his ground and told his mother that whether or not she perceived this agreement, it was true for *him* and that he was no longer keeping it. From that point forward, he would hold nothing back in their conversations—he would include her in all the details of his life.

To my knowledge, Dorothy never outwardly acknowledged that the agreement had existed. However, she did change her behavior toward Tom and became more tolerant of his lifestyle. In time, she even began talking to his partner and spending time with the two of them.

Why is it necessary to talk over your agreements with the other person to change him or her? Because there's a good chance that the other person is holding you to your agreement. He or she expects you to keep your end of the bargain, and when you don't, he or she may try to influence you not to change. If you put others on notice that you aren't keeping the old agreements, you encourage yourself to change and may also limit the other person's efforts to prevent that change.

Sam had never been close to his four children. He felt he had been a good father, but as they had entered their teenage years, he seemed to be unable to communicate with them. It wasn't really a bad relationship—it just wasn't much of a relationship at all.

When Sam began to realize his agreement with his children ("If you don't tell me about your life, then I won't criticize how you live it") he became desperate to change it. He truly loved his children and grieved over the loss of their companionship. His own stern façade was the result, in his mind, of his horrible experiences during the Korean War. Now, he was working hard to break through the emotional wall he had built around himself and to connect more meaningfully with his family.

Sam decided the best way to deal with this was to rent several cabins in a resort town in Colorado—one cabin for each of his children's families. He spared no expense for the weeklong getaway.

Soon after he invited all of his children, the trouble started. His oldest son complained that he didn't want to use his limited vacation time to go on a family reunion. One of his daughters said that it might be too difficult to bring her three-year-old on the plane trip, so she couldn't come.

Sam was devastated. Why were they so resistant? Why were they so unwilling to repair the relationship?

The problem was that Sam had not spoken with them about his discovery of the agreement and how very much he wanted to change it. His children were still operating under the old, unspoken agreement. Why would they want to spend a week with someone whom they felt they hardly knew and with whom they weren't really comfortable?

When Sam realized what had happened, he spent a great deal of time composing a loving and supportive letter to each of his children, apologizing for his part in their lack of a relationship and explaining how he wanted to change that. He explained about the agreement he felt they had both kept and that he was willing to change his part of that agreement. No more criticism of things he disapproved of—he would do his best to be a loving and understanding father to his adult children.

That letter made all the difference. From that day until Sam died six years later, he and his children rebuilt their relationships and discovered that they did truly love each other.

Sometimes, however, the important person in your life with whom you hold an agreement is no longer accessible or alive, as in the case of Carol. Carol's father died when she was nine years old and her mother never fully recovered from the loss. Carol and her sisters grew up with the unspoken agreement that they were always to take care of their mother, since she could no longer care for herself. Later, in her adult years, long after her mother's death, Carol went through a series of marriages, all to men who had serious problems. In each case, Carol had to "take care of" her husband. In time, she would find herself exhausted and resentful from giving so much and the marriage would fall apart.

What is important to learn from Carol's experience is that some agreements are made when you are very young and you subsequently transfer them to the other significant people who come into your life. In Carol's case, she became a lifelong "caretaker" of those she loved. If she wasn't tending to someone else's needs, she felt as if she were useless and unwanted. So time and again she plunged into the role of denying herself and giving to someone else, bouncing from wanting to be needed to resenting being taken advantage of.

These kinds of agreements that extend back to your childhood can be revised and discarded if necessary, but that takes time and understanding. The problem is that these agreements have so embedded themselves in your psyche that to break them, even when you are aware of them, is to create a great deal of anxiety. It feels uncomfortable and vaguely wrong. Only with practice and patience can you begin to undo these agreements and forge a new path for yourself. But remember, *it can be done.*

What is one agreement in your life that you feel needs to be changed or eliminated? Try writing a letter to the person or persons involved explaining the agreement and how you'd like to revise it.

There is one more very important point about agreements you should know: *The anxiety you experience in life is* directly *related to the number of unconscious agreements that you strive to keep.* The more agreements, the more you worry and the more drained you become. Eventually you either sink into the gloom of depression or you explode—throwing away all your agreements and everything associated with them, rather than seeking to negotiate a conscious, healthier agreement.

I remember a client named Kathy who came to see me about her new relationship with a wonderful man. This man was everything she ever dreamed of, yet she couldn't seem to relax and enjoy the relationship. Her list of reasons why this relationship might not work was long and varied:

He's divorced. ("It's wrong to marry someone who is divorced.")

He's too handsome. ("Handsome men always cheat on their wives.")

He has a great job. ("He will probably take off with his secretary.")

He's compassionate. ("Real men can't be kind.")

. . . And the list went on and on.

Almost all of these agreements were made between Kathy and her mother, who had been divorced from a very handsome, successful man who cheated on her when Kathy was quite young. Her mother wanted to protect Kathy from men like him, so she instilled these agreements in Kathy all throughout her childhood. Whenever Kathy dated a boy at school, her mother found something wrong with him and eventually convinced Kathy that he was no good for her. As an adult, Kathy rarely took any of her boyfriends home to meet her mother, but nevertheless, her mother's voice was always present in her mind, nagging and prodding her to find something wrong with the man.

By the time she came to see me, Kathy was ready to dump the whole relationship. Even though she loved her boyfriend, the anxiety it was provoking in her was too great. She had decided that the relationship couldn't possibly be healthy if it caused her that much distress.

I worked with Kathy to understand her agreements and to begin to let them go. Instead of the old, limiting agreements, we worked on a new one: "When I am attracted to a man who is kind and makes me feel like the woman I want to be, I will love him." It took time and a great deal of work, but eventually Kathy was able to release her old agreements and move into a successful, loving relationship. Almost immediately, when she released the old agreements she was relieved of the terrible anxiety that had plagued her through most of her life.

The persistence of unconscious agreements and the effect of them on your life can never be underestimated. I'm reminded of a story that Werner Erhard used to tell often. I think it sums up the power of agreements well.

If you put a rat in front of a bunch of tunnels and put cheese in one of them, the rat will go up and down the tunnels looking for the cheese. If every time you do the experiment you put the cheese down the fourth tunnel, eventually you'll get a successful rat. This rat knows that the fourth tunnel is the right tunnel and goes directly to it every time.

If you now move the cheese out of the fourth tunnel and put it at the end of another tunnel, the rat still goes down the fourth tunnel. And, of course, gets no cheese. He then comes out of the tunnel, looks the tunnels over, and goes right back down the cheese-less tunnel. Unrewarded, he comes out of the tunnel, looks the tunnels over again, goes back down the fourth tunnel again, and again finds no cheese.

Now the difference between a rat and a human being is that eventually the rat will stop going down the fourth tunnel and will look down the other tunnels, and a human being will go down the tunnel with no cheese forever. Rats, you see, are only interested in cheese. But human beings care more about going down the right tunnel.[1]

Why do we care about going down the *right tunnel?* Because we cling to agreements that tell us to do so. How we are educated, when and whom we marry, what we do for a career, how we raise our family are all products of our agreements. Whether they are agreements with our parents, society, God, or our spouses, we structure our lives around those agreements and do everything in our power to keep them.

The right tunnel isn't always the one we've agreed to go down. The right tunnel is the one with the cheese. It is the marriage that is loving and supportive, not the one that you hoped would work but didn't. It is the job that is fulfilling, and maybe not the one that only gives you prestige. It is the life you truly want to live, not the one you were expected to live. The tunnel you agree to go down is the one you think will most likely reward you, but if that doesn't turn out to be true, what is the point of continuing to go down the same path? Why cling to that agreement?

We are often faithful to our agreements to a fault. Letting go of those agreements can be extremely difficult, especially if you've held them for most of your life. The more ingrained the agreement, the more difficult it is to release it.

If you find yourself saying, "But I can't let go!" you're not alone. Every one of us feels that way from time to time. Let me give you a little parable to think about:

Once a man was walking through a forest thinking about his tendency to always feel angry.

"I just don't want to be angry anymore," he kept thinking to himself.

Deeper into the forest, he saw the wise sage of the forest standing by a tree—actually had his arms wrapped around the tree.

"O great sage," said the man, "can you help me? I've been plagued with anger all my life, and I just can't stand it anymore. Can you give me your teaching?"

"I can certainly help you," said the sage, "but first I have to wait until this tree lets go of me."

"But, sir," said the man, "the tree isn't holding on to *you, you're* holding on to *it.*"

The sage smiled. "That is my teaching," he said, and let go of the tree and disappeared into the forest.[2]

Letting go of old agreements is never easy, quick, or painless. Letting go is never a single decision—it is a series of decisions made one after the other, day by day, to consciously release old mental habits. Sometimes we must slowly pry our own fingers, one by one, from their suffocating grip around our own neck.

The first important step toward resolving a crisis is to examine carefully the agreements that you keep. Your inability to resolve a crisis and the persistent need to avoid, run away, deny, or medicate it away is based in those agreements. The crucial riddle you must solve here is: What agreements might be preventing you from facing a suppressed crisis?

To help you focus on the agreements that may be holding you back, try an exercise that many people have found helpful. Make a list of the agreements that you hold (you might use the worksheet you just completed as a starting point for your list). Take that list and put it somewhere private but where you will see it every day. You might tape it inside your desk drawer or inside your medicine cabinet. Make a habit of reading those agreements every day. When new agreements occur to you, add them to the list. As you do this, you'll find that your priorities become very clear to you, and more important, you'll begin to discover the agreements that have outgrown their usefulness and may need to be changed or discarded.

Trances We Live

We've got one more stop to make before we look at the specific crisis you are experiencing. At this point it's important for you to understand the process you've been using to suppress your crisis.

You suppress a crisis by evoking a *trance*. If the agreements are a barrier that keeps you from confronting your crisis, a trance is the tool you use to avoid feeling it at all. A trance doesn't involve any hocus-pocus; it is simply a way of escaping reality. When you invoke a trance, you simply create a state of consciousness that allows you to escape from the reality of your crisis for a while.

The only way you can live with an unresolved crisis (and remain sane) is to induce a *trance*. You tell yourself over and over that it doesn't matter, that you don't have to confront the crisis, and if you ignore it, it might just go away.

Believe it or not, you are the best hypnotherapist you have ever known. Seriously, you can put yourself into a trance faster, deeper, and longer than anyone else possibly could. You know how to induce the right trance and you do it without even thinking about it.

How many times have you induced the sugar trance when you needed to feel good? Or the "cleaning the house" trance when you needed to avoid thinking about something or finishing a project that is overdue? Or the sex trance when you wanted to stop feeling the pain of your relationship or wanted to forget the frustration of your job?

The list of trances you use is long and varied. You use them so often and so effortlessly, you may not even realize what you're doing. What you are doing is *altering your state of consciousness.* A trance is the process of narrowing your focus and limiting your perceptions, and when you induce a trance, it makes you feel less pain.

The ironic thing about a trance, however, is that it doesn't just limit the pain—it also limits the joy you feel. For example, when you use sex to forget about the office for a while, you may feel some pleasure, but it's nothing like the pleasure you feel when you are fully engaged with your lover and enjoying the full experience. Because you've used a trance to forget your pain, in the same act you are limiting your pleasure.

Trances aren't necessarily bad. They are a gift from nature and help you function in life. At those times when full awareness is too painful or too tiring, a trance helps you escape momentarily and regain your strength so that when you return to full awareness, you are better equipped to deal with reality.

Where the real trouble starts is when you *live in a trance.* That's exactly what you must do when you use a trance to handle an unresolved crisis. You must close off part of your heart and mind so that you can't feel the pain of the crisis. Just like a hypnotherapist, you must continually repeat suggestions to yourself. You must tell yourself over and over again, "It isn't so bad," or, "It isn't my fault," or, "It will get better tomorrow."

To maintain the trance for long periods of time, you must surround yourself with people who will help maintain it. They listen to your repetitive conversations and agree with your limited perceptions. They help maintain the artificial reality of your trance.

When you refuse to confront a crisis in your life, you are forced to maintain a trance to protect yourself. Much of your psychological energy becomes diverted to the trance and you have little time or interest for anything else. In time, the trance starts to control your life.

As long as you are maintaining the trance, you can't begin to resolve your crisis. You've shut down that part of yourself, fearing that the crisis is too difficult for you to handle.

A big step in resolving a crisis is to break the trance. How do you do this? Well, it isn't always easy, especially if you've been practicing the trance for a long time. In fact, the longer you've been living in a trance, the more difficult it is to break it.

Sometimes, your world will break the trance for you. Your spouse walks out. You get fired. Your child gets into serious trouble. These are difficult times when suddenly the harsh reality you've been avoiding comes rushing toward you and overwhelms you like a tidal wave of oppression. You may have panic attacks or feel desperately ill. You may even go so far as to think about ending your life. The trance is suddenly broken and the harsh light of reality is glaring at you.

That's the triggering event we talked about earlier that makes a crisis inflamed. Something happens that breaks the feel-good spell you've tried to cast over yourself. Suddenly, you're face to face with a monster.

But you don't have to wait for a traumatic event to break your trance. A more gentle way of breaking the trance is to take control of it yourself, before your world falls apart. You have created a life that has a steady rhythm, one that is tuned toward maintaining your trance. Just like the swinging watch of the hypnotists of the past, you have given your life a distinct rhythmic pattern that helps to keep you numbed to reality.

To break the trance, you need to stop the rhythmic routine. Stop arguing with your wife every evening. Stop complaining about your child's unwillingness to obey. Stop switching jobs. Stop changing boyfriends every few months or years. Stop working eighteen hectic hours a day. Stop the rhythm that keeps you in the trance.

Whatever activity it is that you see yourself repetitively doing, find a way to stop doing it. You'll be amazed at what will happen. First, you might panic. Then, you might get bored (another kind of trance). If you stick with it and refuse to adopt another rhythm, you'll find that you have no choice but to examine your life carefully.

Be warned! The first things that will emerge after you give up the trance will be your unresolved crises. Like the creature from the black lagoon, those crises will rise out of the shadows of your life and give you grief. You'll want to run and hide in the safety of another trance. But if you stay tuned in to reality and remain honest with yourself (instead of remaining in the fantasy world of your trance), you will get through it and resolve the crisis. That's what this book is all about.

MARGE'S TOO-BUSY-FOR-HER-OWN-GOOD TRANCE

Marge was a good friend of mine whom I rarely saw. She was an attorney and had worked her way up the corporate ladder to become the vice president of human resources for a major entertainment company. Even though we saw each other only a few times a year, Marge was always a delight to be around.

Earlier in her life, Marge had been a married housewife in San Diego, California. When her husband ran off with another woman, Marge quickly found herself looking for a job to support her and her daughter. She went to work as a legal secretary and attended law school at night. After years of truly hard work, she graduated top of her class, and shortly thereafter, passed the California bar examination on her first try.

The memory of being destitute after her marriage fell apart never left her and fueled a raging fear within her. She was determined to do whatever she could to never be broke again.

Marge's passion was for trial work, but corporate law offered her a steady paycheck, so she opted for the legal department at a major retailer in California. She worked all the time and quickly rose through the ranks to become head of the legal department and eventually both the legal and human resources departments. It was only a matter of time before she became known for her competence and hard work, bringing numerous offers from other companies. Eventually she accepted the top human resources position at one of the largest entertainment companies in the world.

Fifteen years after her first husband left, she had consistently worked for twelve to eighteen hours every day, first in law school and later as she was working her way up in the organization. Along the way, she married a wonderful man, Steve, whom she had met at work and who was also an attorney. Marge loved Steve and truly wanted to make the marriage a good one, despite the fact that they barely saw each other during the week and only spent weekends together when she wasn't working or traveling for work.

After a few years, however, Steve grew increasingly frustrated at Marge's manic work schedule. He worked hard too, but he also wanted to spend time with Marge on evenings and weekends. She never gave herself enough free time for the two of them to really spend romantic time together. It seemed their life together was always on the run.

Marge and Steve went to see a marriage counselor, and Marge admitted that she worked too much and that she really didn't have to. Nevertheless, there was something inside her that kept pushing her to work harder. When she took time off, she couldn't enjoy it because she felt guilty over not being at the office.

A few years later, Marge and Steve parted ways as friends. Even though she loved Steve and did not want a divorce, Marge just had not been able to control her obsessive need to work. Ultimately, she sacrificed her marriage to her job.

Marge was creating a trance to avoid the unresolved crises in her life. She wasn't really following her passion (she'd rather have been a trial attorney than just another corporate "hired gun"), and furthermore, she had never dealt with the fear of being destitute, which was also driving her on. Marge knew about both of these crises and would sometimes talk about them privately (for example, she'd express thoughts of quitting the corporate job and opening a private practice). As those crises burned hotter within her heart and mind, however, she distracted herself by staying busy rather than working to resolve them. For Marge it was too threatening to face those looming crises, so she plunged herself deeper into her work, just like the ostrich in the sand, hoping that it would all just go away.

The truth is that a trance works for a while, as it did for Marge. Her resistance kept her so busy that she didn't have time to worry about much of anything else. But as you can see, eventually it costs a great deal. For Marge, it cost her marriage.

The real problem is that a trance doesn't solve anything; it only delays the pain, and ultimately makes it worse. Look at what it cost Marge: She lost her marriage, has a less-than-close relationship with her daughter, and maintains very few friend-ships because of her obsessive work habits. She doesn't have time or energy left for anyone in her life after exhausting her-self at work. While the trance did dull the pain of her unre-solved crises, it also diminished her life.

There are many trances you might induce to suppress a crisis, and there are specific trances associated with each of the seven crises, which we'll look at in detail later in the crisis chapters. For now, let me tell you about a few that I see often and that are used to deal with every kind of crisis.

THE DRAMA CLUB

There's no better form of distraction than a really wild and crazy *drama*. If there's something you want to ignore, why not create a diversion to take the attention off your problem?

Some people are true stars when it comes to drama. If there were awards given out for the best dramatic distraction, they'd certainly be strong contenders. They create such emo-tional upheaval in their own lives and in the lives of those around them that their real problems fade into the back-ground. If you think about it, I'll bet you've known a few of these dramatic players.

Lori was a great dramatist. Whenever her life seemed to settle down and she was faced with the ordinary day-to-day problems of her life, she would create a grand distraction. She'd break up with her current boyfriend and then hole up in her apartment until her friends came searching for her thinking something terrible had happened to her. Or she'd suddenly quit her job and take an "emergency vacation." One of her best dramas was when she refused to attend her best friend's wedding because she didn't like her friend's fiancé. Before the wedding, she tried to break them up, and when she wasn't successful, she decided to completely boycott the marriage, even though she was asked to be the maid of honor. She even tried to convince their mutual friends to do the same.

Maybe you're thinking, "What kind of person would act like *that?*" Sure, it seems a bit on the crazy side, but take a closer look. Lori didn't think of her behavior as dramatic or extreme. At the time she pulled those stunts, she had convinced herself that they were legitimate reactions to what was happening at the time. Lori didn't realize her reaction to the situation was over the top. She was simply creating a drama to distract herself from the crises that were brewing in her own life.

How many times have you looked back on a situation in your life and thought, "Why did I react so strongly to something so insignificant?" The real reason may lie in some other problem that you were trying to avoid.

Emotional turmoil can be totally absorbing. Drama with your spouse, your children, or your friends will keep your mind and heart busy. Creating a drama, as Lori did when she quit her job, can be a very effective way to distract yourself and to add some excitement to your life. When you're busy putting the basics of your life back together, you don't have time to worry about the deeper crises in your life.

ANXIOUS ATTACHMENT

Another creative trance is *anxious attachment.* Anxious attachment occurs when you form a close emotional bond, either through friendship or romance, and you become emotionally dependent upon that person. Everything—even the smallest of reactions—elicits an emotional response from you. As a result you spend a great deal of time and energy following and interpreting the moods of the other person. If that person seems less than enthusiastic about seeing you, you begin to wonder if he or she is breaking off the relationship. If the person spends too much time with someone else, you begin to think he or she is cheating on you.

When you allow yourself to become totally wrapped up in another person's life and emotions, it takes a great deal of your energy and attention. You are able to put your own crises aside while you totally immerse yourself in the life of another human being.

Jo was anxiously attached to her close friend, Carol. Both Jo and Carol were married and in their early forties. Jo and her husband had wanted children, but they were unable to conceive. Carol, on the other hand, had two children. Over the years, Jo had become completely involved in Carol's life and family. She kept Carol's children after school while Carol worked, and she knew all of their teachers by name. When she and her husband went out for dinner, Jo always invited Carol and her husband to come along.

Whenever Carol decided to do something different, like take a trip with her family, Jo got upset if her family wasn't invited to come along. When Carol decided to join a bridge club, Jo began playing bridge, too, and eventually joined the same club.

When Carol's husband was transferred across the country and they decided to make the move, Jo was devastated. At first she called Carol several times every day until Carol asked her to stop calling her at her new job. Jo slid into a deep depression.

Jo resisted dealing with her own crisis by involving herself completely in Carol's life. By doing so, she could temporarily ignore the fact that her own marriage wasn't working and that staying at home made her feel unfulfilled. Not until Carol moved away and she no longer had the distraction did her own problems come crashing down around her.

STRESS ENVY

Another trance you may induce is *stress.* Stress? That's right, stress. Not a few people keep their lives chock-full of stress so that they don't have time to think about the deeper problems in their lives. They sign up for every possible program at work, and they overcommit themselves to their children's after-school activities. They overextend themselves, all the while complaining about how stressed out they are. Why? Because they are distracting themselves with a "busyness" trance.

For example, take a look around your place of work and find the people who are the most stressed out and over-worked. Now, take a look at their personal lives. A real mess, right? Nine times out of ten, the people who are chronically stressed out at work have put themselves in a situation that is stressful to avoid dealing with their own crises. They're so busy putting out the fires at work, they don't have time to think about their own problems, much less try to resolve them.

Not all stress is a self-created trance, but *chronic stress* almost always is. People who refuse to change their situation and relieve themselves of the stress are actively avoiding something else. Despite their loud complaints, they are clinging to their stress. As difficult as the stress may make their lives, their fear is that dealing with the deeper crisis of their life will be even more painful, so they choose to stay stressed out.

THE PLEASURE PRINCIPLE

Another common trance is the obsessive search for pleas-ure. For some people, this means drinking excessive amounts of alcohol or using drugs. For others, the fixation is on more "healthy" activities, such as extreme mountain climbing or grueling marathon runs. All of these things and many others can bring you pleasure, but when you begin to obsessively pursue them, they become self-destructive. By obsessively pursuing pleasure, you are trying to escape the pain of an unresolved crisis in your life.

Ray is a sex addict. He is an attractive man in his mid-fifties. No matter where Ray goes, whether it be to the grocery store or the airport, he keeps his eyes peeled for women he might ask out on a date. Ray isn't really interested in all the women he dates, just in the momentary escape he feels while he is pursuing a sexual exploit. Once the excitement wears off, he's on to some other woman. Ray is resisting the call of the crises that are brewing in his life.

As sex is for Ray, alcohol, food, caffeine, sugar, and all other mood-altering substances can become avenues of escape. Likewise, exercise, bodybuilding, aerobics, adventure sports, and other forms of healthy living can also function as trances.

When you find yourself caught in the vicious circle of addiction, whatever the substance or activity, you're trying to resist a crisis that is crying out for resolution. When you deal with the crisis, you'll find the need for obsessive activity will diminish.

Clients who are executives often tell me about the "consolation prizes" they use in their pleasure trance. These clients buy exotic things like sports cars or big houses, not because they really want them, but because those purchases made them feel better about the tradeoff they've made in their lives. Because these executives have often abandoned their passion and talent for jobs that paid well and gave them powerful positions, they try to silence the boiling crises within by making big, flashy purchases or by taking increasingly exotic vacations. The sad part is, when the executive returns to work, the newness of the purchase soon wears off and another purchase must be planned. I worked with one very high-level executive who couldn't feel comfortable working unless he had some exciting vacation in the planning stages. Often, before he returned from one vacation, he was already reading and planning for the next.

TRYING TO LIVE ABOVE IT (AND EVERYONE ELSE, TOO)

The last trance we'll consider is that of being hypercritical. One way of avoiding the problems in your own life is to spend your time and energy pointing out the problems in other people's lives while trying to convince yourself that you are better than they are.

Susan always wanted to be a fashion designer, but an early marriage followed by children made that career difficult for her. She had dreamed of living in New York and working with all the top models, swathing them in rich fabrics she designed.

Now, she was a suburban housewife in Virginia, outside Washington, D.C.

Susan dealt with her abandoned career by becoming supercritical of what her friends did with their lives. She developed a biting sense of humor and often used it to criticize the accomplishments of those around her. Whatever she did or purchased, it was always "the right thing," and she usually found fault with what her friends did.

A hypercritical mentality is a sad form of resistance that will in time destroy relationships. Everyone knows some older person who has become bitter over the years and criticizes everything that other people do. Eventually, others stay away from them as they grow even more bitter in their loneliness.

Should you find yourself always focusing on the negative aspect of other people, it's time to stop and ask yourself why. Why do you have such a need to point out their faults? What are you obsessed with what everyone else is doing wrong?

The old adage is absolutely true: When you point a finger at someone else, three others point back at you. When you are motivated to criticize other people, it comes from the frustration in your own life and the crisis you haven't resolved.

Which, if any, of these trances have you been using?
How have you distracted yourself from the inner work
you know you need to do?

FOUR STAGES OF EVERY CRISIS

Breaking the trance is just the first stage of resolving your crisis. There are four distinct stages of every crisis. They are:

1. Breaking the trance
2. Confronting the crisis
3. Sorting through the confusion
4. Resolving the crisis

In the *confronting the crisis* stage you allow yourself to hear the real question that the crisis asks of you. Every crisis has at its core a question about who you are and how you are living your life. It is this "crisis question" that you've been avoiding by suppressing the crisis. Only when you really allow yourself to hear the question and are willing to search for an answer are you confronting your crisis.

For example, remember the story of Don the executive from the first chapter? It wasn't until Don had lost both his job and his marriage that he finally allowed himself to hear this question and consider it for himself.

Don had been on the fast track for most of his life. When he finished high school, it was just expected that he would go to college. Once in college, he married and it was just expected that he would get a good job after graduation. Don never had time to explore himself and discover what he was really all about. Instead, the practicalities of his life ruled him, and like a good workhorse, he put himself to the task.

The problem was that Don never allowed himself to confront his crisis of "What is my passion?" Every year that went by, he was more invested in his job and career, regardless of whether he really enjoyed it. With every pay raise came a new expense—a new house, a car, and children—so there was no room for him to question his passion.

But even though Don thought he hadn't the time to explore his passion, the crisis remained. The question was seeping through every area of his life, making him discontented and frustrated. He began seeking thrills in other areas, such as trips to Las Vegas and affairs with other women. Eventually, this unresolved crisis caused him to lose his marriage and his job.

At this point, Don finally began allowing himself to hear the question his crisis was asking of him. All the obstacles that he had put in the way of discovering his passion had now been removed. Crisis has a funny way of doing this—when you put up excuses to deny the crisis, it has a way of removing those obstacles.

When Don finally allowed himself to "hear" the question, it didn't seem to make things any easier. Just imagine how he felt. He had twenty years of his life, not to mention the years of college, invested in something that he wasn't even sure he liked. He had made those choices based on the expectations of others. What was the driving passion of his life? He wasn't sure, but he did know it probably wasn't what he had been doing.

Don finally came around and discovered the crisis question that had been hounding him all these years, and where did that lead him? Straight into *sorting through the confusion,* the third stage of crisis. It wasn't clear to him what he should do, and he began to question everything about his life.

The confusion stage is when you truly realize that you don't have a clue to the answer to the crisis question. It is when you reluctantly admit that you don't know what your passion is, how to have a deeply loving relationship, or what is the true meaning of your life in this world. All you know during the confusion stage is that you want to find some answers.

The confusion stage is extremely uncomfortable. You lose your bearings. For Don, he knew he didn't want things to continue as they were, but didn't have a clue which way to go. His old ways had failed him, and he didn't have a firm grasp on a new way. What was he to do?

The confusion stage is necessary to growth. As the award-winning research of scientist Ilya Priogine proved, confusion is critical to all living systems. What Priogine discovered in his research on thermodynamics is that a certain amount of disequilibrium and disturbance is necessary for a system to avoid deterioration. Priogine's work asserted that dynamic systems don't seek equilibrium. Rather, they constantly maintain a state of nonequilibrium, keeping the system off balance so that it can change and grow. In other words, a certain amount of confusion is *necessary* for a system to avoid entropy and for it to grow.

Another important discovery comes from the study of chaos and systems. What scientists and mathematicians have discovered is that there is always an order to be found in chaos. Margaret Wheatley writes, "Chaos has always had a shape—a concept contradictory to our common definition of chaos—but until we could see it through the eyes of computers, we saw only turbulence, energy without predictable form or direction."[1]

What all this means is that a period of chaos is *always* the precursor to a new order. Think about what happens in countries where the system of government fails. What happens next? Chaos—and then a new regime rises to power. What happens after a devastating earthquake? Confusion—and then a new landscape begins to emerge.

The lesson that history teaches is that confusion is a necessary precursor to growth and development. Why should it be any different in your life?

Life isn't neat, orderly, and predictable. If you try to make it so, you will spend much of your life in frustration and anger. Life is a system that oscillates between order and chaos—every swing toward chaos births a new order. That's how all life evolves.

So even though confusion is painful, it is essential. To avoid it is only to increase the pain, not to diminish it. Remember, within your confusion lie the seeds to a wonderful breakthrough. It happens every time.

The next stage of crisis is *resolving the crisis,* and it can only happen after you've allowed yourself to wander about in the confusion stage. You won't resolve your crisis of passion until you've given yourself the opportunity to experiment with opportunities. You won't resolve your spiritual crisis until you've allowed yourself to explore various spiritual paths. You won't resolve your crisis of individuation until you relinquish old attitudes toward your parents and allow yourself to figure out what it is you really believe apart from them.

In many ways, the resolution stage is an act of faith. It is the point where you finally begin to trust the evolution in your life and allow it to carry you forward. You let go of the preconceived ideas and expectations and allow your life to evolve naturally, on its own. In other words, you begin to let go and *trust the process.*

Let's return to Don's story. Don spent a great deal of time in the confusion stage—almost six months. When he finally emerged, he had come to peace with his new life and finally relinquished any thoughts he had of returning to his old career. At this point, he was open to whatever opportunities might emerge.

This was where the fun started. Don began doing things he'd never allowed himself to do before. He'd always admired old cars that were restored, but he'd never allowed himself to own one, much less acquire the skills to work on one. He bought an older convertible that caught his eye and began restoring it. Much to his surprise, not only was he good at it, he found the work was a real joy. He couldn't imagine why he hadn't allowed himself this pleasure before.

Don wasn't looking at his newfound hobby as a career option. He was simply exploring his interests and following where they led him. He didn't know what tomorrow would bring, but he was beginning to understand some very essential things about himself. His interest in the old convertible had no objective—it was pure fun.

In the year that followed, Don's life moved from confusion to the last phase of crisis, *resolution*. Don's resolution began when he was offered the opportunity to co-own a small car restoration business. Don contributed the business know-how while his co-owner had the mechanical expertise. Don took his savings, invested it in the garage, and went to work. Today, Don owns a thriving business that he loves, has remarried, and is more content than he remembers ever having been before.

IS IT MEANT TO BE?

There is a right direction for your life, and crises are the signposts pointing the way. If you tune in to the direction they offer, you can put your life back on track.

This may be hard to understand, so let's take a look at how nature keeps all things on their proper path. Take for example, your body. Unless you're suffering from a disease, you don't worry about having the proper hormone levels in your blood or the right amount of antibodies to fight off infection. Why don't you worry about this? Because your body cares for itself naturally. Your body continues to function perfectly without intervention.

So it is with your life. You contain everything you need to evolve into a happy and fulfilled person. So why aren't you experiencing this? Because you intervene in this process and in so doing, block it. Your life starts to look and feel confused, so you deliberately change the course of your own evolution. When you do, you land yourself squarely in trouble. One of the primary ways you intervene in your own evolution is by clinging to old, outdated agreements.

The acclaimed psychologist Carl Rogers liked to compare the process of "living fully" to his beloved garden. All he needed to do was make sure the garden got plenty of sun and water, and the earth and nature did the rest. Carl only set the stage for optimal growth: He didn't control, manipulate, or create it. He had to *trust the natural process.*

In this age of the aspiring individual, we often feel we must *do* something to make our evolution into happiness occur. The key to avoiding this pitfall is when your life begins to seem chaotic (the beginning of a crisis), rather than springing to action, sit back and look for the new emerging pattern. Just as it is in the mathematical science of chaos, even the most chaotic of situations has an emerging pattern. It only looks confusing because you've never seen this pattern before.

That's how we grow in the best direction—by paying close attention to the patterns that emerge and listening to the direction those patterns offer. All too often we try to direct our lives with some preconceived ideas about what we should be or do, when what we *really* should do is follow the natural unfolding of our lives.

Crisis is natural and it is a *very* strong message about a new and emerging pattern. Are you listening to the message? Think about Don. His crisis was a clear sign to him that his life had swerved way off course. Sure, he could have continued with the old career, trying to keep his marriage together, and meeting the expectations of everyone else, but that wasn't his natural evolution. What Don really needed to do was follow his passion, which meant owning his own restoration garage. Once that was in place everything else began to fall into perfect order. He moved from his crisis to a wonderful breakthrough.

Do you want to know what is "meant to be" in your life? Take the time to stop and really look at what is happening around you. What patterns are emerging in your life? What crisis is constantly dogging you? You can visit all the psychics and astrologers of the world, but none can give you clearer direction than the signs that are in your life right now. You've got all the direction you need to find your highest good—all you must do is pay attention. Breakthroughs happen naturally, if you are willing to deal with the root causes of your crisis. Breakthroughs are the result of your listening to and learning from the natural pattern of your life, rather than trying to control and manipulate what happens to you. Just like Don, you too can have the breakthrough you need. There's no better time to start than right now.

Reflect on your recent history. Do you see any patterns emerging? Can you envision those patterns leading you somewhere?

In the next section of the book, we'll begin with a short quiz that is designed to identify the current crisis that is troubling you. After you complete and score it, you can choose to read about all the crises or you can go directly to the crisis that is of most concern to you now.

Whatever the repeating pattern you are experiencing, whether it be a cycle of broken relationships, addictions, career dissatisfaction, depression, weight loss or gain, or anxiety, it can be traced to difficulty that you are having in resolving one of the seven basic crises. Each of these issues is a symptom of the deeper, unresolved crisis.

To start you on your way to a breakthrough, let's take a look at the crisis that is holding you back. . . .

The Seven Crises

Before you begin reading about the seven crises in detail,
complete the following quiz and follow the scoring instructions. This brief quiz will tell you which of the fundamental
crises is unresolved and creating difficulty in your life.

For the following statements, put a check in the white box
next to the statements that describe how you feel most of the
time (ignore the shaded boxes). Don't take too much time
with any one statement. Go with your first feeling about each
statement and keep moving until you reach the end of the
inventory.

	A	B	C	D	E	F	G
If I made more money, I might be happier.	X						
What other people think about me is very important.		X					
If I would only work harder, I'd be more successful.	X						
I'm not certain that I have any real talent.			X				
I'm uncomfortable when I act solely on my feelings.		X					
I often feel out of control of my life.					X		
Much of my life as it is today is so because I tried to do "the right thing."	X						
I've always thought of home as where my parents live.				X			
I rarely feel inspired.	X						
I don't believe in anything beyond what I can see and touch.						X	
I wish I had a meaningful reason to get up and get going in the morning.		X					
It's dangerous to dream.			X				
I will recognize the love of my life when I first meet him/her.		X					
My education (or lack of it) has always held me back.			X				
Other people aren't interested in hearing about my troubles.		X					
Sometimes I get very angry and later wonder why.					X		
There are some things about myself it's best not to share with others.			X				
I usually consider my parents' feelings when making decisions about my life.				X			
My lover must also be my best friend.		X					
Ultimately, I'm not sure there is any meaning to life.						X	
I often feel lonely.		X					

	A	B	C	D	E	F	G
Life doesn't turn out the way you wish it would.	■	■	■	■	■	■	
What I do for a living I do because I've done it for a long time.	■	■		■	■	■	■
The world is often a dangerous place.	■	■	■	■		■	■
I'm always trying to improve myself.	■	■		■	■	■	■
Most of my beliefs about life come from how I was raised.	■	■	■		■	■	■
I envy people with talent.	■	■		■	■	■	■
Religion is something you are born into.	■	■	■	■	■		■
If I were smarter, I'd be more successful.	■	■		■	■	■	■
If I don't live my ultimate dream, my life has been a failure.	■	■	■		■	■	
I am haunted by my childhood.	■	■	■	■		■	■
It's important that my parents approve of how I live my life.	■	■	■		■	■	■
Science will ultimately disprove the spiritual.	■	■	■	■	■		■
I am often angered by injustice.	■	■	■	■		■	■
I worry that other people will take advantage of me.	■	■	■	■		■	■
Part of growing up is learning that dreams usually don't come true.	■	■	■	■	■	■	■
I often resent my parents.	■	■	■		■	■	■
Pleasure is all the joy there is in life.	■	■	■	■	■		■
I try to accomplish what my parents wanted to do, but were unable to do.	■	■	■		■	■	■
I must accomplish my dream, or I will always be unhappy.	■	■	■		■	■	■
I sometimes think about dying and it scares me.	■	■	■	■	■		■
I am a failure because I am not famous, successful, rich, etc.	■	■	■	■	■	■	■

	A	B	C	D	E	F	G
TOTAL							

Now, for each column (A, B, etc.), tally up the number of white boxes you checked. For example, you may have checked anywhere from zero to five white boxes in column A. Write the total of each column in the TOTALS row. Now look at the totals you have written. Which columns have the highest number of checks? These columns represent the crises that are most pressing for you. Consider reading the chapters that correspond with these columns first. They are:

A. The Crisis of Passion (I Want to Feel Inspired)

B. The Crisis of Contact (Who Will I Share My Life With?)

C. The Crisis of Self-Confidence (Why Can't I Believe in Myself?)

D. The Crisis of Individuation (How Can I Become My Own Person?)

E. The Crisis of Fear (I Want to Be in Control of My Life)

F. The Crisis of Spiritual Meaning (What Does It All Mean?)

G. The Crisis of Broken Dreams (This Isn't What I Dreamed It Would Be)

I Want to Feel Inspired

[THE CRISIS OF PASSION]

We move toward a kind of divine presence because, through
our passions, we are utterly present. We are utterly charged
and focused. We are oblivious; we forget ourselves, our
troubles, our day-to-day living-on-Mulberry-Street lives. We
hitch ourselves to something bigger.
—GREGG LEVOY[1]

I could best describe Sue as apathetic. She was friendly,
even jovial at times, but underneath that thin veneer, there
didn't seem to be much feeling there. It was as if she were
there, but not there. Something was missing.

Sue had raised two children, and once they had both
entered high school, she had returned to her career as an
emergency room nurse. She had a good marriage and a supportive family that was very close. She had a good life—but
something was missing. What was it?

That's the question she brought to therapy. "What could possibly be missing in my life? I have it all, but I'm haunted by the feeling that something isn't there that should be. I feel as if life is somehow passing me by."

Sue had spent much of her life being a good girl. She was a good daughter to her parents. She was a great wife to her husband. She was the exemplary mother to her children. Sue had strong convictions about the "right thing" to do and she lived her life accordingly.

So what could possibly be the problem?

Somewhere long ago, in the rush to be the honor student, to have a good career, to raise a family and be a loving wife, she had lost touch with her passion. Passion? She knew about the right thing to do, but not about passion. The idea of passion seemed vaguely naughty to her—isn't that something that leads you down the garden path only to find heartbreak?

If it was sex we were talking about, she told me, "Don't worry about that. I have a very fulfilling sex life." No, it wasn't sex we were talking about. It was *passion*.

Passion is the one idea that is strong enough to inspire your entire life. It isn't an activity or a person; it is an *idea*. Passion is the one meaning in life that is worth living for, or even dying for. Passion is what ultimately gives your life meaning.

"Well, I raised my children and I love them dearly. They give me great joy," Sue said one day in therapy. "I think raising children must have been my passion. Now that I've done that, I guess there's not much left for me."

I pushed Sue to go a step further. "What is it about raising children that so inspires you?"

All I got in return was a blank stare, and eventually, a few words about how important children are to a full life. I agreed, but wouldn't let her off the hook. "What is it about children that truly inspires you?"

Sue left my office confused and agitated. She later told me that as she left my office that day, she decided never to return. This therapy business was supposed to make things better, right? Well, so far, it was only making things worse.

Fortunately, Sue returned the next week, only because, I suspect, she felt it was the right thing to do. After all, she had agreed to work with me for at least six weeks before deciding whether to continue. It was only week four.

"I don't know about this passion stuff," she said as she smoothed her skirt. "It just doesn't seem that important."

"But you did come here because something is missing in your life, right?"

She agreed.

"So let's pursue this passion thing for a bit longer, okay?" She just glared at me.

"Tell me what you think passion is," I asked.

"I really don't know, and believe me, I've thought about it a lot this week. I'm no artist or hero, if that's what you mean. I'm just a mother and wife, isn't that enough? I take care of my family and I love my husband. I don't understand why you seem so bent on making me feel bad. Passion is for those who want to throw away their lives on cheap thrills. I think it leads to nothing but trouble. I promised myself I would make something of myself, and never turn out like my father. Look where passion led him . . ." And the tears began to flow uncontrollably.

Over the next few sessions I learned all about her father. He was, by definition, a dynamic man. He was a Baptist evangelist—a minister who traveled from church to church, preaching revivals that sometimes went on for months. He was totally consumed with winning as many souls for the Lord and the Baptist Church as he could.

During much of Sue's childhood, she rarely saw her father. She and her mother would often receive long letters from him, usually from some place deep in the rural South. They were always about how the Lord was moving upon people and convicting them of their wicked ways. He would be home soon, he would always write, but rarely did that come to pass.

Sue secretly wondered why the Lord needed her father to save all those souls and never allowed him to be at home. Why didn't the Lord provide more money for them, so she could have the things the other kids at school had? Most important, the other kids had a mother *and* a father who lived at home. Why couldn't she have that?

Sue deeply resented her father's passion for saving souls. She longed for a regular family that stayed at home and had regular jobs with weekends to play in the park or take drives in the country. Somewhere, sometime long ago, Sue had decided that was the kind of family life she would create for herself when she grew up.

Sue and I worked together for several more weeks before we really began to understand why she couldn't seem to feel passion. Not only had her father been an evangelist, he firmly planted within his children the idea that their feelings were bad, even sinful, and would lead them down a path of destruction and ultimately jeopardize their souls. If they enjoyed something too much, it was probably sinful and should be avoided.

So Sue never really explored what might make her truly happy, and instead focused on doing the right thing for herself and her family. So many years had gone by that she couldn't remember being really passionate about anything.

Sue did remember being really excited while she was in nursing school teaching other women about how to care for their newborn babies. She really felt alive when she was helping other women take care of themselves and their children.

Over the next weeks, we explored this experience and began discussing ways in which Sue might once again try teaching. She tried various things, like teaching Sunday school at her church and helping out at the local elementary school on health day. None of these things seemed to bring back the spark of that early experience.

Then, one day, an opportunity fell into her lap. An old friend had started a training business that helped newly graduated nurses to pass the licensure exam. Would she be interested in teaching a few of these test preparation courses? As it turns out, that was just the experience Sue needed. She taught one program and then another. Before she knew it, she was hooked. She loved working with these women, helping them to consolidate all that they had learned in nursing school. Sue was a dynamic and entertaining teacher and the students loved her. In time, she expanded her programs to include courses for women who were newly single and needed help with things like building a credit history, completing their taxes, and getting a mortgage. These were all the things Sue had done for her family for years, and it gave her a great thrill to share them and help other women get on their own feet.

The last time I saw Sue, she was like a different woman. Vibrant and excited, she seemed very alive—a far cry from the woman I had met just a year earlier. She had quit her job at the hospital, which paid a good deal more than what she making from her seminars, *and she was truly happy.*

Like Sue, many of us have never really allowed ourselves to discover our passion. Instead, we were caught up in the current of life and all the activities that go with it. We were too busy keeping our agreements and meeting the expectations of those who were important to us to really discover what it was that *we* wanted to do. As the years went by, we so distanced ourselves from our passion that we believed we weren't passionate about anything at all.

What you're left with is the feeling that you've somehow missed out on life. You feel as if life is passing you by and as if you aren't doing anything that really matters. Eventually, this can make you feel as if your life has little meaning, and you may be led to question the purpose of it all.

This is when you need to take a break from life and rediscover your passion. It's there all right, but it's been buried under years of neglect and denial.

Your passion will lead you to places you truly never imagined, to the only places where your soul can truly be fulfilled. Sometimes it has even led people, quite contented, to the point of risking their own lives. Consider the story of Mark Dubois.

Mark was a river guide on the Stanislaus River in Northern California. The Stanislaus had given Mark many gifts over the years—a job, friends, a peaceful retreat—but its greatest gift had been an awakening of Mark's passion for the environment. His love for that river stirred deep within him something he had known as a little child—a wonder and respect for nature.

In the mid-1970s, the California legislature approved plans to build a dam on the Stanislaus and create a large reservoir for the growing water demands of the area. Key to that plan was the construction of New Melones Dam.

Mark, a six-foot-eight mountain man, was no politician, but his passion for the environment and saving the Stanislaus drove him from his comfort zone in the hills to the halls of the state capital in Sacramento, where he lobbied heavily against the dam. For years he fought the project with no success. In the spring of 1979, the New Melones Dam was completed.

One small success Mark had won was a compromise between the environmentalists, politicians, and Corps of Engineers: The water in the reservoir was to be raised no higher than the old bridge at Parrott's Ferry. Even at that level numerous old beaches and archeological sites would be covered by water, but others would be spared.

But as so often happens in politics, once the engineers began filling the reservoir, they decided to take the water level higher than they had previously agreed. When word got out that this was happening, Mark and the organization he founded, Friends of the River, began writing letters to protest to the Corps of Engineers, the state legislators, and even the White House. In his letter, he stated, "I plan to have my feet permanently anchored to a rock in the canyon at the elevation of Parrott's Ferry the day the water reaches that elevation. I urge you to do all in your power to prevent the flooding of the canyon above Parrott's Ferry."

And that's just what he did. Gregg Levoy writes that "on the appointed day, not unaware of the terrible irony of possibly being killed by the very river that had called him, he kayaked to a remote spot on the rising reservoir, weeping much of the way there—not out of fear but grief—and chained himself to a large boulder, having first hidden a key well out of reach. He had only a sleeping bag, a poncho, some books, and a cup to scoop water from the reservoir, which was only two feet below his perch (and rising). Mark told only one friend—dubbed Deep Paddle—where he was so that he could bring him news. Mark told him that if the water reached his knees not to come back."[2]

Fortunately for Mark and the surrounding environment, the engineers agreed to stop filling the reservoir just before it reached Mark's knees. The river hadn't been saved, but Mark had limited the damage, and he felt he had done his best.

Mark's stand against the Corps of Engineers by risking his life touched many people, and in the years that followed, Mark was given many opportunities to work for the saving of the environment in various places around the world. Today, Mark is the director of Worldwise, a campaign to ensure that the international loans made by the World Bank and the International Monetary Fund contain conditions that protect the environment in developing countries. It's a long way from when, in his cut-offs and tee shirt, he stood in the river guiding tours of its many wonders. But this is where Mark's passion has led him and he feels that he would have it no other way. How could he have planned such a career? How could he have opened all those doors? He couldn't have, but his passion did it for him.

Mark has never made much money for himself by lobbying. In fact, there have been times when he had to use his personal savings to fund his environmental work, but that doesn't bother him in the least. Sure, there are times when he'd like to be making the kind of money other high-powered lobbyists make, but then, they are only "hired guns." Doing his part to save the environment is worth more than money could buy for Mark.

Mark is not different from you or me, except that he was willing to follow his passion 100 percent. Nothing less would have achieved the same results.

This is the paradox of your passion, and it is at the crux of this crisis. If you discover your passion and refuse to follow it, or if you are only willing to follow it halfway, you have doomed yourself to a greater misery than having never known passion. Imagine if Mark had loved the river as he did, but was unwilling to go out on a limb and lobby the legislature or chain himself to a rock for it. Where would he be now? We can only imagine—unemployed, bitter, obsessed with the "old days," angry at the forces that "stole" the river from him. Mark's life illustrates a truth that has been proven time and again: *Your passion demands no less than all you have to offer.* If you give it anything less the results can be devastating.

When you discover your passion and taste its sweet nectar, you are changed forever. You *must* write the book, sing the song, dance the dance, climb the mountain, or start the business. You will have no choice if you wish to be fulfilled.

> *What inspirational idea / activity / practice have you pushed aside in your life?*

The personal reward for following your passion is guaranteed—success is not. Mark wasn't successful in blocking the building of the dam, remember? Your book may not be published, or your business may fail. There are no guarantees of success, only the promise of fulfillment.

The famous New Orleans sculptor Enrique Alferez has spent his entire life of ninety-four years pursuing his passion for sculpting. Despite his recent fame and prosperity, for most of his life he was a poor artist, struggling to get by in the French Quarter. Sounds a bit romantic, doesn't it, following your passion alongside the likes of Tennessee Williams and William Faulkner?

Looking back at his life, here's what Enrique has to say about those romantic notions:

> You've heard people talk about the artists in the French Quarter in the '30's, haven't you? How exciting it all was to be creative then, how romantic it was to be living an artist's life? Well, you know what all that is? I'll tell you: it's bullshit, that's what it is.
>
> Artists have to do their work like anybody else, and that work ain't easy. When it's done, you may be proud of it, or you may not be. It may sell and it may not. People may like it or they may hate it. And sometimes you even have to defend it.[3]

Whether your passion is art, protecting the environment, cooking, or whatever it is that really turns you on, it's hard work to stay true to it. What's more, there are no guarantees of monetary success. Most passionate people, just like Enrique, spend most of their lives struggling to make ends meet.

Seems like risky business, right? You bet. But there's one important point you must burn into your heart. When you follow your passion, there is no failure. Sure, the business may fail, no one may join your cause, or you may lose the election.

These are not failures when they are born of passion—they are extremely important experiences for your development into the person you want to be. They are *opportunities despite the outcome.*

Maybe this sounds a bit clichéd, like making "lemonade out of lemons" or something equally trite, so let me explain this by telling a true story.

ROLLING IN DOUGH

For most of Tom Monaghan's life he's been consumed with a passion for one simple thing: selling pizza. Tom loves everything about the pizza business from the ingredients to the smell of it baking to the challenge of delivering it hot.

Tom's story begins in 1960 when he was a college student. It was then that he and his brother Jim borrowed $900 to open a pizza parlor near the campus of Eastern Michigan University. When Tom wasn't in school, he lived at the pizza parlor, doing every task himself—from making the sauce to scrubbing the floor. His brother Jim, on the other hand, had a full-time job at the post office and spent far less time at the parlor. Eventually the disparity between their contributions led to Jim's selling his half of the business to Tom in exchange for a 1959 Volkswagen Beetle that the business used as a delivery car. The loss of the car was a real setback for the business, but Tom was determined to make it work.

To keep the business afloat, Tom dropped out of college. Quickly he discovered that he couldn't keep working eighteen-hour days and that he needed help, so he went looking for someone who knew the pizza business. In time he discovered a man who had successfully run his own pizza delivery business and who was interested in a partnership with Tom. For the small sum of $500, Tom gave him a 50-percent stake in the business.

Tom and his partner decided to expand the business and opened two more stores and a full-service restaurant. After a couple of years, Tom discovered that his partner was taking advantage of the business, spending money on cars and property. Nevertheless, Tom remained loyal to the partner, thinking the business needed his partner's experience.

Eventually, the partner became very ill and deep in debt to hospitals and doctors. Since their partnership was so entangled, the partner's pending bankruptcy threatened to close the business. Ultimately, it cost Tom $75,000 to pay off his partner's debts, for which he was legally liable.

For most, that would have been the end of the road. But it wasn't for Tom. He was determined to succeed in the pizza business. The next year, while paying off the bankruptcy debts, Tom managed to make $50,000 in net profits.

All seemed to be going well, and then disaster struck again. In April 1967, a fire wiped out his anchor store, destroying $150,000 of equipment for which the insurance was only willing to pay $13,000. Amazingly, Tom was more determined than ever and found a way to finance the losses. Within a few years, not only had he recovered from the fire, the pizza parlor, now under the name Domino's, had grown to a dozen stores and had a dozen more in development. After nearly ten years of working eighteen-hour days, seven days a week, it all had paid off. Tom had the pizza business he had always wanted.

But it was too good to be true. Once again, everything went south. Tom had expanded the business too fast and accrued $1.5 million in debt. Now, Domino's faced bankruptcy, *again*.

"We had overexpanded and added new stores to territories before the first stores were fully established," Tom said. "We also made the mistake of sending in untrained managers with no experience to run the new stores and overstaffed our home office."

On May 1, 1970, Tom lost controlling interest in the company. The bank took over the company and kept Tom in a figurehead position as president. The new owners closed unprofitable stores and cut back on the staff. Tom's only responsibility was to run twelve corporately owned stores.

After ten months with the new ownership, Tom arranged to buy back control of Domino's in exchange for a few franchises. Once he was back at the helm, a number of his franchisees were angry about his return and filed a class action antitrust suit against Domino's. According to Tom, this was truly the lowest point in his life.

Over the following nine years, Tom refused to give in and slowly built the business back, paying off all the old creditors. As if all this wasn't enough, he simultaneously won a trademark lawsuit brought by the manufacturer of Domino Sugar.

Today Tom has built Domino's into the largest home delivery pizza business in the world. Because of his passion for the business, Tom persisted long after many would have thrown in the towel. Owning 97 percent of Domino's, Tom became one of the wealthiest self-made people in the country.

The story of Tom Monaghan and Domino's is one of being consumed by passion and learning the lessons passion has to offer. By giving himself over to his passion, he found unlimited energy that propelled him through extraordinary obstacles. Every time disaster struck and more rational voices advised him to quit, he held on to his dream and eventually out-succeeded them all. Tom says of this, "I feel all these setbacks were tools for me to learn from. I used them as stepping-stones and didn't see them as failures. A failure is when you stop trying and I never did that."[4]

Pizza was Tom's reason to live. For more than ten years he lived in a small apartment with nothing but a bed and kitchenette. When he traveled for business, he would often sleep in his rusty Rambler to save money for the business. Tom's passion wasn't delicate or contained. It was bold, rough, and uncontrolled. By giving himself over to this passion, he found the one source of unstoppable energy within himself that wouldn't quit until success was his.

Was Tom ever afraid of failing? You bet. Was he ever discouraged? More than once. He refused to give in to the voice of fear. Rather than heed those misguided whispers, he allowed his passion to guide him.

The story of Tom and Domino's pizza is filled with great highs and a few devastating lows. But no matter how hard the roughest parts of the road, it was the road to fulfilling Tom's true purpose in life.

ONE SMART COOKIE

Debbi Fields is now famous for her cookies, but that wasn't always the case. On August 16, 1977, she opened the first Mrs. Field's Chocolate Chippery in Palo Alto, California. During that entire first day, she didn't sell one twenty-five-cent cookie. With a twenty-five-thousand-dollar bank loan at 22 percent interest, her first weeks in business were anything but exuberant.

The words of her business advisor had begun to ring true: "A cookie store is a bad idea. Besides, the market research reports say America likes crispy cookies, not soft and chewy cookies like you make."[5]

But Debbi refused to give up. She had always wanted to have a baking business (at thirteen she took a job as the Oakland Athletics' first female foul-line catcher in order to earn five dollars a week for butter, sugar, and flour), and she wasn't going to let go of her dream so easily.

So, she started giving away the cookies. She walked the street with a platter of cookies, giving one to anyone who would take it, and before the end of the day, she started a sales increase that didn't stop until she had built a $425-million Mrs. Fields' Original Cookies global empire.

During all of her business dealings, she raised a family and made sure that she always attended her children's events and made dinner every night. "I am a zealot about dinner. No matter the sports activities, always have dinner together. I make that an absolute priority."[6]

Then, during the 1993 economic downturn and the "over-malling of America," Debbi had to sell some of her share in the business to keep it afloat. It was painful to give part of the business to someone else, but she had no other choice if it were to stay in operation. "I had to be responsible, to make sure everyone would get paid."[7]

Difficulty is as much a part of passion as is success. Does this surprise you? It shouldn't. Think about every person you've known who has wholeheartedly followed his or her passion. Were they immediately successful? Were they always happy about the results they were getting? If your friends are like most people, you'll definitely have to answer "no."

Think about all the images we have in our culture of passionate people. They almost always involve some level of suffering for the sake of passion: the starving artist/writer, the religious martyr, the athlete in training, the businessperson climbing the corporate ladder, and the door-to-door campaigning political candidate. These are just a few of many pictures we have of passionate people trying to follow the difficult road to their dream.

There is probably no more dramatic picture than comes from one definition of passion found in the dictionary: "The sufferings of Jesus in the period following the Last Supper and including the Crucifixion."[8] Could there be more suffering and triumph contained in any one story?

If passion also brings suffering, why follow your passion? Because the alternative is even worse—a life of regret, frustration, and apathy. We saw in an early chapter that there is no avoiding pain in this life, and following your passion is no exception. It will certainly bring you great joy—even ecstasy—but there is a price you will pay. Here's the most important part: Talk to anyone who is following his or her passion and he or she will tell you the joy and fulfillment is *more* than worth the cost.

> *Are you afraid that following your passion will cost too much? What do you imagine the cost to be?*

CONFRONTING YOUR PASSION

By now you're probably asking yourself, "Where did I lose my passion?" Or maybe you're wondering, as I once did: "Do I have any passion?"

Not to worry. You've got lots of passion—it's just lying dormant for now. Before you can move forward, however, you've got to first be willing to break the trance that you've created to block the pain.

The trance you use to protect yourself from the crisis of passion is the trance of apathy. Because you are afraid of the strong feelings of passion that live just beneath the surface of your awareness, you tell yourself that you don't feel much of anything. Rather than acknowledge and deal with the feelings, you force yourself to feel nothing.

Why do you fear your passion? Because you have the vague notion that it might lead you to radically change your life as you now know it. Over the years, you've slowly built a life that is practical and secure, but is it passionate? Sometimes the path of security leads away from passion. You are terrified that if you let those feelings "out of the box" you won't be able to control what happens. You might do something that others see as stupid or foolish. You might have to completely reevaluate the choices you've made throughout your life.

So rather than open the Pandora's box of passion, you simply close the door on any strong feelings. You don't allow yourself to become emotionally invested in anything. You create a life that is mundane and devoid of feeling. You do what is expected and you play the role you've created for yourself. You're the good wife, the supportive husband, the loving daughter, or the dutiful son.

The problem is that in the night when you're alone and quiet, you crave passion. You daydream of something exciting and real—something that makes your heart pound and gives you a real reason to get out of bed in the morning. You miss the feeling. You miss the joy and sorrow that comes, too. You watch movies and read novels to try to live through someone else what you've forbidden yourself to live, and it satisfies the craving long enough to get through the night.

You can't live without your passion. You can exist, maybe even function, but you can't truly live without passion. The first step to rediscovering your passion is to break the trance of apathy.

To help you break the trance, let's take a look at some of the unnatural agreements you've made with yourself and others that help support your trance of apathy. Many of these are agreements that you first created as a child. Your parents, teachers, ministers, and other well-meaning adults passed on to you some faulty agreements about life that they, in turn, learned from their parents. On the surface, these agreements seem to be commonsense truths, but in reality, they are dangerous lies that taught you to abandon your passion. They are so insidious that I like to call them the Five Agreements That Will Kill Your Passion. Here they are:

1. Money Will Satisfy You

Many of us live as if money is the only thing that matters in this world. We hang on to jobs that we hate just for the money. We live across the country from family and friends because of an offer for more money. More than a few of us have even destroyed our marriages because we were hell-bent on making money. The deep-down agreement is that more money, perhaps just a little bit more than what we now have, will make us happy. So we abandon our passion for the pursuit of money and all it can buy.

Money, no matter how much, doesn't satisfy. Warren Buffet, one of America's wealthiest people, is convinced that money doesn't make anyone happier. In a recent interview with University of Washington business students, Buffet emphatically stated that what makes him happy and fulfilled is that his work is *exactly* what he wants to do. He even went so far as to say that he regularly turns down lucrative business deals when they require him to work with "people who make his stomach churn" or because they involve some business that doesn't interest him. Buffet is so convinced that money won't make anyone happier (and can make one's life appreciably more difficult), he is leaving 99 percent of his considerable fortune not to his family, but to society. To Buffet, this is one of the most loving things he can do for his family.

Think of the people in your life who are the most fulfilled. Are they the wealthiest people you know? Probably not. In fact, some of the most fulfilled may not have much wealth at all.

If you want to be fulfilled, the objective of your life must be to follow your passion, not to amass the biggest possible bank account. Remember: Success is a *feeling,* not a possession.

2. Hard Work Makes You Successful

Of all the gifts our forefathers gave us, the Protestant work ethic is not one of the better ones. In fact, it has destroyed more lives than it has helped. Why?

Working hard at something doesn't necessarily mean that anything good will happen. For instance, if I want a swimming pool in my backyard, I can take out my shovel and dig a hole for it. Seems a bit silly, but I could do it. Or I could rent a backhoe and do the job quickly and with much less effort. Better yet, I could contract with someone who knows how to install pools and will do it with far greater efficiency than I can.

If I should choose to dig the pool with a shovel, I will be working very hard but not very smart. Sure, I'll be busy, busy, busy—but for what? Digging that hole will only occupy my time and keep me from pursuing my real passion (which is definitely not digging an enormous hole).

Hard work pays off only when you first do the inner work of discovering what you want to do, and consequently, are good at doing. When you do that, no matter how hard you work, it doesn't seem hard at all!

In many ways, hard work is like a trance-inducing drug. It tires you so that you don't have the energy to think about what is within you. It temporarily deadens you to the disappointment that your life isn't what you want it to be. As a result, you must constantly keep yourself busy and too tired to think about what you are missing.

In my travels as an author I have met countless people who tell me they have a book they want to write, but can't find the time to do it. They're so busy making money and doing all the other projects in their lives, they are too tired at the end of the day to even think about writing. When I suggest they might rearrange their lives, work a little less, and set aside time to indulge their passion for writing, I get a long list of excuses for why that can't happen. It's really too bad, because these people will never write a book until they are willing to let go of the myth about hard work.

3. You Should Never Get Carried Away

This deeply held agreement—that something terrible will happen if you allow your emotions to express themselves through your actions—causes you to miss much of what life has to offer.

From where does the agreement come? It can come from many places, but often it is the result of something very tragic happening in your family while you were young. Perhaps a death or a divorce occurred. Whatever it was, the feelings of grief and sadness threatened to incapacitate you or your family, so you all agreed to not let your feelings get the best of you. "Swallow it and keep moving" is the motto of this family—and it works in the short term, but it will kill your passion and diminish your life in the bigger picture.

Another prominent place where this agreement started was with our fathers (and sometimes our mothers) who may have experienced World War II, Nazi concentration camps, the Korean War, Vietnam, or any of the other wars around the world. Many men and women were exposed to such horrible circumstances that they learned to numb their feelings and to never let them out. Once again, this is a very effective strategy for surviving the horrors of war, but a terrible way to live. Sadly, these parents are often very uncomfortable with their children's emotions and teach them that their emotions are dangerous and should never be trusted. As a result, many of us grew up agreeing that we would never let our feelings carry us away.

But being "carried away" is an essential part of the passionate life. Think of all the great people throughout history, or better yet, someone you know who has accomplished something of meaning in his or her life. Didn't he or she get "carried away"?

George Washington got carried away . . .

Susan B. Anthony got carried away . . .

The Wright Brothers got carried away . . .

Eleanor Roosevelt got carried away . . .

Martin Luther King, Jr., got carried away . . .

Ella Fitzgerald got carried away . . .

Jesus got carried away . . .

Buddha got carried away . . .

The list could go on and on. The point is that you never really reach your full potential until you get "carried away." When you allow your deepest feelings to surface and energize your life, you find the momentum that carries you into your greatest accomplishments.

Of course, the term "carried away" is really a misnomer. That you give credence to your feelings doesn't mean that you are wildly out of control. It simply means that you've found a dynamic source of power within yourself and that you've allowed that power to invigorate your life. Even when you're "carried away," you're still very much in control of your actions.

4. An Idle Mind Is the Devil's Workshop

Sitting quietly with nothing to do has become a rarity in today's world. In fact, our modern culture seems to despise quiet solitude. It seems lazy, inefficient, and nonproductive.

This is blatantly untrue. In fact, quiet time for reflection and meditation is *essential* to being happy. Your mind and body require a time of quiet to rejuvenate and refocus. Without it, you slowly deplete yourself until you lose touch with your inner voice. You forget who you really are and what you want out of life and instead choose to vibrate with constant busyness. Your actions lose meaningful direction, and you become adrift in the sea of your own life.

Many of us made the agreement in childhood that we wouldn't be lazy. Every family has some good-for-nothing lazy bum, and you probably heard stories about all the problems this person encountered. Somewhere along the way, you agreed never to turn out to be lazy and have all those bad things happen to you.

As a result, quiet time elicits guilt within you. You feel useless and as if you *should* be doing something productive. You need to train yourself to let these feelings go. Sometimes the most productive time you will spend is in quiet solitude, clearing the decks for that one great idea to come forward in your mind.

When you take the time to block out all the noise of the outer world, you strengthen the sound of your inner voice. In those times of silent contemplation, you retune yourself to the deep meaning of your life. You are then reminded of your purpose and passion—the two essential ingredients of your own greatness.

5. If It Isn't Broken, Don't Fix It

Sometimes, it is just when everything is sailing smoothly that it is time for change. Why? Because uneventful times often mean that for some reason we have stopped growing. And, like everything else in the universe, when we're not growing, we are dying. Life is a process of change, not a stagnant experience of consistency. Nothing in this world stands perfectly still. As the business writer Judith Bardwick has aptly written, "There is danger in the comfort zone."

Many people agree to never change—and the results are always disastrous, for no one stays the same even if he or she tries. You hear this all the time: "You're not the person I married." "You're not the person I hired." "You're not the child I raised."

A rich life of passion is a life of constant change and growth. When you stop growing, you begin to lose touch with your passion. Passion is always about movement and never about holding tightly to the past.

Each of these unnatural agreements will prevent you from living a life full of passion. They say:

"Hold back."

"Fit in and don't make waves."

"Be wary of your emotions."

"Live your life to meet the expectations of others."

Like shedding an old skin, you must shed the old agreements that have blocked you from knowing and following your passions. Those old ideas have kept you from creating the life you have always dreamed you could have by blocking your passion and thereby blocking you from discovering the richness of life that is possible.

What unnatural agreements are stopping you from following your passion?

CONFUSION

The big question still screams, "What is my passion?" If you're like most people in the middle of this crisis, you don't have the foggiest idea.

And that's how it should be. You're experiencing this crisis because you've neglected a very important part of yourself—your passion. The longer you did this, the more out of touch you became. Now, the idea of passion may seem unclear and may even be totally absent from your life.

The old agreements that you have kept prevented you from exploring those areas of your life where passion resides. But luckily it's still there, just waiting to be discovered.

Sitting back in your armchair and trying to figure out your passion is *absolutely the wrong thing to do*. Passion isn't mental—it's emotional and spiritual. The only way you'll ever discover it is by *tasting, smelling, feeling,* and most important, *DOING*. Passion is explored, not conjured up in your mind. Passion is an experience, not a thought.

Let's try an exercise to help with the confusion you're feeling right now. Take a piece of paper and draw a vertical line down the middle of it. That line, starting from the bottom of the paper going toward the top, is your life. The bottom is your birth and the top is where you are now. Take some time and mark on that line the significant events of your life, such as graduating from school, getting married, getting divorced, suffering the death of a parent, and giving birth to a child.

Now that you've divided your life into segments according to the significant events that have happened, write into each segment the things that most interested and inspired you during that period. Don't leave out any segment, especially not your childhood.

I Want to Feel Inspired

Here's how one woman completed this exercise during a seminar:

Significant Events	Interests and Inspirations
Today	????
Susan was born.	Love being a mother.
Married Bob.	Began entertaining (dinner parties, etc.). Quit work and loved traveling with Bob.
Started work as publicity director.	Liked feeling financially independent. Liked working with different kinds of people. Enjoyed arranging big events.
Graduated from high school.	Wrote poems/published one in senior yearbook. Enjoyed theater classes and acting in school productions. Spent lots of time with college sorority.
Born on August 14, 1955.	Loved to take ballet classes. Enjoyed being in Girl Scouts. Worked on school yearbook staff.

Now look back over your list. How many of the things that once interested you have you done lately? How many of these things did you abandon along the way?

It's true that many things that once interested us no longer do so now. The important point in this exercise—and it is extremely important to explore your passion—is to uncover the themes that run through these activities. These themes are the key to rediscovering your passion.

Let's look at the worksheet on the previous page. This woman has several clear themes that run throughout her life. She loves being part of a group of people. She also seems to love expressing herself creatively—as seen in her love of writing poetry and the theater.

Those themes will lead her to her passion, but only if she *acts* upon what she has learned. Perhaps she could start out by joining the community theater, by attending a local writers' group, or by volunteering at the local library to read books aloud during the children's hour. Maybe none of these activities will ignite her passion, but they will definitely lead her in the right direction. What she learns from her experience in these activities will help her to refine her exploration and move closer to doing something that is truly inspirational. If she continues with this, there is no doubt that she will rediscover her passion. The key is: *Keep moving.* You'll never find your passion sitting in that comfortable armchair!

Passion is experiential. If you want to discover a soul-stirring reason for your life, *you must broaden your experience.* Only by trying many things will you actually discover the one key to your inspiration.

How have you experienced passion in your life?

RESOLUTION

Reaching the resolution phase of a crisis, as we have seen, is a leap of faith. It is resolving to follow what you've learned about yourself, regardless of the consequences.

Resolution in the crisis of passion comes only when you are willing to follow your passion wherever it leads you.

There is a huge difference between wishing that some thing about which you are passionate "falls into your lap" and actually following your passion where it leads. The first approach is passive and doomed to failure. The second approach will dramatically and positively change your life.

You must make your passion your intention. Not your wish. Not what you admire in others. Not what you read about. Not what you dream about. You must *intend* to follow your passion if you want to resolve this crisis.

The best way to have a good idea is to have many ideas. The best way to be a successful entrepreneur is to open a business. The best way to write the great novel is to write a novel. The best way to be a consultant is to start consulting. You must make passion your intention if you want to experience all the joy it has to offer.

This doesn't mean that all the doors will fly open for you and everyone will meet your passionate intention with welcoming arms and wallets. In fact, it may lead you directly into a few failures. Discovering your passion is no guarantee of financial success—it is a guarantee of successful living.

Van Gogh never got anything but poverty from his paintings, yet they are strong evidence that he lived his passion. Edgar Allan Poe died in rags and was buried in a pauper's graveyard. At the height of her fame, Judy Garland didn't have enough money to pay for her own meals or hotel rooms. Look at the founding director of almost any nonprofit that is truly doing a needed service for the community and you'll find someone who hasn't gained financially by following his or her passion for service. Money and passion are only *sometimes* bedfellows.

Sometimes we must make planned detours on the road of passion. In the arts it's called a "day job" and it's what you must sometimes do to take care of your physical needs while you follow your passion.

Planned detours can take many different forms and are almost always necessary. Maybe your detour is to go back to school and earn the credentials you need, or maybe it is working extra hours while living simply so you can save enough money to quit your job and follow your passion. Perhaps it means volunteering to answer phones at a local charity so you can learn about how the organization works. It might even be as drastic as selling your home and buying something smaller so you don't have to work as much and have more free time to give to your passion.

One of the biggest blocks to resolving the crisis of passion is resistance to taking a detour. One client of mine, Robert, was a likable fellow in his late twenties. Robert came to me broke and frustrated. For the past eight years he had changed jobs, at the very least, twice a year. It seemed that every one of those jobs had the same problem—it was a dead end.

What was happening to Robert wasn't a run of bad luck; it was his resistance to starting at the bottom of an organization. When he worked for a landscape company, he felt he should be doing the work of landscape architect, not digging holes and hauling fertilizer. When he worked for a telecommunications company, he felt he should have a desk job, not be selling beepers door-to-door.

Even when Robert really liked what he was doing, his frustration over being "low man on the totem pole" got the best of him and he would quit. Wasn't there anyone who could see his potential for success?

That you have a passion for something doesn't mean you can start at the top without working your way up. That you love to cook doesn't excuse you from having to make the same loaf of bread twenty times a day after you open your own catering business. In time, your passion will shine through and allow you to hire someone else to deal with minutiae of the job. Until that time comes, it's up to you to take the detour.

How can you make your passion your "intention"?
What detours might be necessary along the way?

BREAKTHROUGH

The final resolution in your crisis happens when you experience the truth that "the only investment in my life that will pay off is an investment in passion." Nothing else is worth the investment of your life but passion. Nothing.

A close friend of mine, Sharon, is now a well-known motivational speaker. Sharon suffered a great deal of her life with an unresolved crisis of passion. She struggled for years, floundering in job after job, until she finally took a position in an advertising firm that required her to make presentations to clients. At first, her presentations were scripted and delivered in a rather stilted style, mostly because her boss insisted that every word of the presentation be approved before delivery. Trying to be a good employee, Sharon never veered from the script, even when she thought she could do better by being more spontaneous.

Several years after she took the marketing job, her boss took an extended leave of absence. During her boss's absence, Sharon was to make several presentations to various clients. Since her boss wasn't available to review the scripts, Sharon decided to do one without writing every word of it beforehand. The result was a stunning performance and kudos from everyone in the room. They couldn't believe how Sharon had changed for the better. The CEO of the advertising firm even called Sharon's boss to congratulate him on whatever he had done to help Sharon do so well.

Sharon remembers that presentation well. She remembers

how she was flooded with confidence as she began to see her audience respond to her words. She was thrilled with the response and remembers a definite feeling of having found her niche in life. From that day on, Sharon never presented from a script and went on to become a very successful and highly sought-after speaker.

Sharon's breakthrough came when she realized the passion of her life: public speaking. In that moment, she knew that was what she was meant to do, and that it was something that she would continue to do for the rest of her life. While public speaking is exhausting to some people, Sharon is actually energized by it. Her whole demeanor changes when she steps up to the podium, and for hours afterward, she continues to feel a remarkable surge of energy. Sharon found her breakthrough.

When you are willing to step out in faith and resolve to act on your passion, there will come a moment when you realize that you have found the one thing that has the power to inspire your entire life. You will realize that there is nothing else you want to do more. It is an undeniable moment of joy and excitement. When it happens you will know it, and never again will you search for your passion, because you will have found it.

How can you begin acting upon your passion **today?**

The Four Stages of the Crisis of Passion

1. Breaking the trance of apathy

You create a trance of apathy—having no strong feeling for anything—in order to avoid dealing with the fact that you are suppressing your passion.

2. Confronting the crisis

You acknowledge that you haven't allowed yourself to explore and experience passion.

3. Sorting through the confusion

You aren't certain that you are passionate about anything, but you are starting to have some ideas of the things that inspire you. You cast about, trying and tasting different experiences.

4. Resolving the crisis

You discover and experience what really excites you. You relentlessly focus on it and make the decision to follow wherever it leads you.

Who Will I Share My Life With?

[The Crisis of Contact]

Goals for Me

I want to love you without clutching,
appreciate you without judging,
join you without invading,
invite you without demanding,
leave you without guilt,
criticize you
without blaming,
and help you without insulting.

If I can have the same from you
then we can truly meet and enrich each other.
—Virginia Satir[1]

Why can't I feel something deeply for another person?
Why do all my relationships feel muffled and somehow dead-

ened? Why am I bored with the people I love? Will I ever feel that overwhelming sense of aliveness and emotion that I felt the first time I fell in love, or experience that thrilling sense of connection and understanding I had when I made my first best friend?

The crisis of contact can happen whether you've just been through a painful breakup or are still in a relationship with someone you love. It is a crisis about breaking through the emotional walls of everyday life and experiencing honest contact with other human beings. Whether you're recoiling from a traumatic breakup or simply lulled by the rhythm of everyday life with the same person, you are craving emotional contact.

You need, crave, and seek emotional contact—the strong feeling you had the first time you fell in love. You want not just another person to be near you, but someone to be near and to *know* you—your deepest desires and dreams. You yearn for someone to help you through the tough times and help you to stand after a fall. You hunger for someone to celebrate your life with you.

The complete, unabridged, and unedited story of your life burns within you to be shared with another person, and the weight is too much for you to bear alone. You need a fellow traveler on your journey through life.

You can surround yourself with people, yet feel utterly alone. You can fill your social calendar and still feel isolated—maybe even alienated. You can be married and feel virtually unloved. You can be part of a large family, yet feel unshakably like an orphan.

There is only one way to satisfy your craving for emotional contact, and that is through complete *emotional honesty.* Uninhibited and uncensored honesty about what you feel, who you really are, and what you really want is the secret to making contact, and thus finding satisfying emotional contact. No partially honest or partially revealing substitute will satisfy you.

Emotional honesty is not easy. You may fear that if you completely reveal yourself to someone else, he or she will reject you. If you tell that person that you are sometimes bored, sometimes frustrated, even sometimes disgusted by him or her, perhaps he or she will be hurt and withdraw. What good does that accomplish?

Actually, quite a lot. Revealing your true self, especially the parts that you imagine others might not like, can be threatening. The way you protect yourself from this feeling of threat is by telling yourself that it isn't right to hurt another person's feelings. If I tell him that I don't want to have sex, he'll think I don't find him attractive. If I tell her that I'd rather not spend the day with her, she'll think I don't want to be her friend. If I tell him that it makes me uncomfortable when he acts that way, he'll leave me.

So where's the good in these true confessions? They are the things that make up the truth of you. Who you really are, not who you want others to *think* you are, is the basis of satisfying emotional contact. When you create an image of yourself (which is exactly what you are doing when you hide your true feelings), you are actually withdrawing emotionally. The relationship becomes partially artificial and, as a result, it isn't satisfying.

The truth is that when you hide your true feelings in order to "spare" the feelings of others, you're really not concerned about the other person but about yourself. You are concerned that if they know how you really feel, they will withdraw from *you*. The real concern is not the consequences of the truth to other people, but the consequences of that truth to you. The person you are really protecting is yourself.

Perhaps this sounds like an argument for complete rudeness and selfishness. It isn't. When you are emotionally honest on a regular, day-to-day basis, there are no surprises or hurt feelings from others. They know who you are and how you feel. You respect them enough to reveal your true self to them, and that is never hurtful. It may disappoint them that you feel a certain way, but there is no betrayal or painful surprise.

It is partial emotional honesty that creates the barriers in your relationships, barriers that dull your feelings and make them less satisfying to you. Even though you may love someone, you will not feel that sense of being "in love" again until you reach a place of emotional honesty. If you have been through a traumatic breakup and are unwilling to trust another person again, you cannot feel that deep feeling of romance and excitement. You will only go through the motions, but will not have the experience.

How do you create emotionally honest relationships that will satisfy you? To begin answering this, we've got to look at the kinds of relationships you need. More specifically, you need three different kinds of relationships in order to be fulfilled: *lover, confidant,* and *mentor.* To understand what emotional honesty looks like and how you can create it in your life, we must look at it in the context of each of these relationships.

It probably isn't surprising to you that having a lover is important to lifelong fulfillment. In fact, most of us grew up believing that having a lover *was the only* intimate relationship we truly needed. We believed that all other relationships were secondary to that of finding "the love of our life."

That's where the trouble begins. You go on a search for one person to fill your need for emotional contact when what you really need is three different people. You look for a lover to fill your need for romance, companionship, and mentoring. It's an impossible task that you set out to complete, and as a result, you spend much of your life dissatisfied with your relationships. If you are lucky enough to find the one person who fits all three roles, you eventually destroy the relationship by demanding too much of one person.

Are you surprised by this? Have you always assumed that a true lover *must* also be your confidant? If so, read on, because understanding the difference between these two types of companions will help you resolve this crisis and satisfy your hunger for emotional contact.

A lover is a participant in your life. He or she is intimately involved with you and a cocreator of your life. Your lover becomes a player in your life story, influencing and, at times, changing the plot. You confide in your lover and hold no secrets from him or her.

So how is a lover different from a confidant? A confidant is someone to whom you can tell the story of your life as it evolves. Rather than being a central *participant* in your life, he or she *reflects* your life back to you. Certainly a confidant is a meaningful part of your life, but he or she isn't closely involved in the same way that a lover is. While your confidant knows your deepest secrets, he or she usually isn't the subject of those intimacies. Confidants retain some objectivity and, consequently, the ability to challenge and clarify your life's story for you.

Think about a romantic relationship you have had that eventually ran into trouble. Whom did you turn to for help and advice? If you did turn to someone, it was most likely your confidant. Your confidant helped you to see the situation more clearly and to make choices that supported your well-being. Perhaps your confidant even helped you to heal or, if necessary, dissolve the relationship. That's what confidants do for one another. A true confidant complements and enhances your relationship with your lover.

This isn't to say that your relationship with your lover doesn't need to be completely open and honest—it does. The right lover for you is the person to whom you can completely and honestly reveal your soul. That said, you also need someone else to whom you can reveal yourself: someone with whom you are not as vulnerable, and someone whom you trust, but who isn't deeply involved in your life. Having a confidant in no way infringes upon the honesty and openness you share with your lover—it complements it.

Many people mistakenly believe that having a confidant somehow diminishes their relationship with a lover. Not only is this a faulty idea, it is a certain recipe for trouble. You hunger for another perspective on your life. You need to tell someone about your relationships, your joys, your failures, and your frustrations. A confidant is someone whose judgment and friendship you value; a lover is someone to whom you are attracted and with whom you wish to share the experience of your life and love. *You need both a confidant and a lover in your life.*

For example, a husband who dearly loves his wife may find a confidant in a colleague at work or a friend at the gym. A devoted and fulfilled wife may find a confidant in her best friend, whom she talks with on the phone every day.

Some insecure lovers will not allow their partners to have a confidant. They believe that any relationship that shares honesty outside the romantic relationship is a threat, and they actively work to sabotage and undermine their lover's confidant relationship. In the end, not only does this diminish the intensity of their relationship with their lover, it creates dissatisfaction and can ultimately lead to the breakup of an otherwise loving relationship.

Have you ever tried to make one person fill the role of lover and confidant? What happened?

ACROSS THE ROOM

After years of owning her own travel agency in Boston, Jackie fell in love with one of her male customers. It was a whirlwind romance that ultimately led to marriage, and Jackie sold her business and moved to an island off the coast of Florida to live with her husband. Back in Boston, Jackie had a very dear friend who had been her confidant for many years. Unfortunately, the miles between them and their radically different lives caused their relationship to wane. Jackie missed her friend dearly.

Ten years after the marriage and her move to Florida, Jackie came to see me. Something was missing in her life, but she wasn't sure what it was. She loved her husband and they shared a wonderful life, but still she felt something was missing.

Jackie described it this way: "When I'm at a party, I want to look across the room and see my best girlfriend. When our eyes meet, we'll both know exactly what the other is thinking and feeling. I miss that connection. I really miss having a best friend."

Jackie's yearning for a confidant made her wonder at times if there was something wrong with her marriage. After all, if she really loved her husband, shouldn't that be enough to satisfy her?

In our work together, Jackie was able to find comfort in knowing that there wasn't a thing wrong with her marriage and that it was normal—even desirable—to crave the companionship of a confidant as well as a lover. She could, and should, have both. Her task wasn't to fix her marriage but to allow herself to develop the kind of friendships that might lead to something deeper and more meaningful.

A great deal has been written and said about finding the right lover, but precious little is mentioned about the critical importance of also finding a confidant. Let's take a closer look at this essential part of fulfilling your need for emotional contact.

Maybe you've been thinking, "I've got good friends. Aren't they my confidants?" Good friends are wonderful, and you're lucky to have people in your life who love and cherish you, but they aren't the same thing as a confidant. A confidant is someone special—someone with whom you develop a deep sense of trust and understanding. A confidant is someone to whom you can say *anything* without fear of losing his or her companionship. Friends may share your life, but they often don't share the deepest secrets of your soul. They only know the part of you that you choose to show them—and they love you for what they know.

Why are you driven to share yourself completely and honestly with another person? It is a necessary process of purging your mistakes, honoring your victories, and ultimately validating your life's story. It makes you *feel* much more alive when you share your experience of living with another person. It allows you to shift the heavy load of carrying your own life. Having a confidant is absolutely necessary for peace and contentment.

You may have different confidants at different times in your life. Given the great investment of time and trust involved, most people have no more than one or two, and usually not at the same time. Letting go of an old confidant is so painful, and the cost of developing a new one so great, most people can't do it more than a few times in their lives.

Confidants not only listen to and understand your life experiences; they can challenge you, even to the point of anger, like no one else. The reason for this is simple—confidants know your deepest fears and your greatest shortcomings. Because they are onlookers to your life, they can often see with a clarity that eludes you. Sometimes they tell you what you already know deep in your heart, but don't want to acknowledge—and especially don't want to hear from a friend.

But this is precisely why you hunger for a confidant—to challenge you and ultimately to validate your experience. You need to know that someone else knows the complete story of your life and isn't horrified or disapproving. He or she knows exactly who you are and hasn't rejected you *for being you,* and that experience is incredibly empowering and liberating.

DEANNA FINALLY FINDS A CONFIDANT

Deanna was a professor of anthropology at the local university. She spoke in a deliberate, methodical tone, as if she were delivering a lecture. She had plenty of friends, she said, most of whom were associated with the university, but none with whom she felt really comfortable. She had a bridge partner and they played every week, but she rarely talked with her about anything other than the game. She also had a boyfriend whom she loved dearly, but still she was overwhelmed with a sense of alienation and loneliness.

She told me how much she wanted someone she could really talk to. Someone who didn't expect her to be the expert or have all the answers or want something from her—just someone who would listen and understand. That's why, she said, she came to therapy.

But over the course of six months of therapy, Deanna complained that her feelings of needing someone to talk to weren't being satisfied. Talking to a therapist just wasn't the same as talking to a good friend.

I encouraged Deanna to explore ways to develop new friendships—perhaps she could find one that would become what she was looking for.

Interestingly enough, none of the new friendships she began cultivating helped her feel better. They all seemed too surface and the people she chose were too preoccupied with their own lives to really develop into true friends.

One day Deanna told me that she was renting out the basement of her house to a former graduate student, Jan, who was down on her luck. Jan had been a good student, but the job market for anthropologists was tight and it was difficult for a new graduate to get a job. She needed a cheap place to stay while she worked part-time and looked for a job.

After Jan moved into the basement apartment, Deanna and Jan began a habit of having dinner together several times a week. When Deanna wasn't seeing her boyfriend and Jan was free, they would spend the evening cooking pasta and talking over glasses of wine. Deanna felt at ease with Jan.

Deanna and Jan couldn't have been more different. Deanna was raised in Berkeley, California, by parents who were highly educated and wealthy and expected a great deal from their children. Jan was from a small farming town in Iowa and was the first in her family to finish college, much less earn a graduate degree. They were twenty years apart and for the most part held two very different perspectives on life.

One evening, after a particularly troubling phone call from her twenty-year-old son, Deanna had dinner with Jan. During the dinner, she told Jan something she hadn't mentioned to anyone else. Eric, who was adopted, had been very troubled since he was a young child. Now Eric, who was going to school in New York, had decided to begin the two-year process of becoming a transsexual. Eric had informed her that he no longer would be called Eric, but Elizabeth.

Deanna was in tears. How would she ever tell this to her parents? What would her colleagues think? What if Eric wasn't thinking clearly and years down the road regretted his decision? How would people treat him, knowing he was once a man? What kind of life could he possibly have?

Deanna and Jan talked until the early hours of the morning. Deanna had never allowed herself to be so brutally honest with another person. She had always held back and kept the deepest secrets to herself. This time, she opened up completely.

In the years after Deanna and Jan spent the night talking, they became the closest of friends—confidants for each other. Even after they both married and moved to different cities, they continued to know each other's lives completely and help each other through the difficult times. While they didn't always agree, they both deeply cherished their friendship and it still continues today.

FINDING A CONFIDANT

Where do you find a confidant? Who shall it be? How do you find this person?

A confidant is someone who listens to you and accepts you for who you are. A confidant will sometimes challenge you, but not reject you. Very often, they're not the person you might expect to develop such a close bond with. Here are just a few examples of the confidant relationships of people that I have known:

♦ Don, a busy high-tech executive, found a confidant in a part-time caddy at the local golf course who also is a teacher of severely mentally impaired children. While they seemingly have nothing in common, they understand each other better than if they ran in the same circles.

◆ Martha, a young stay-at-home mother, found a wonderful confidant in her elderly neighbor across the street. Several times a week, they sit down for coffee and talk. Even though they are at different points in their lives, they complement each other. The neighbor is able to help Martha see the bigger picture when she is overwhelmed by the day-to-day stress of raising three children, and Martha brings a feeling of hope, youthfulness, and vitality into the elderly neighbor's life.

◆ Joan, a retired schoolteacher and mother of four, found a confidant in the nun who serves at her local Catholic church. Even though their lives have had a very different focus, they are able to understand each other's joys and sorrows.

Would any of these people have *expected* to find a confidant in the person they did? Probably not, but they were open to the relationships that developed in their lives and, as a result, found what they never expected to find.

Do you have a confidant? What can you do to begin developing or enhancing your confidant relationship?

WHO WILL BE YOUR MENTOR?

Like that of a confidant, the third essential intimate relationship is an often-neglected one that is necessary for your own fulfillment. You need to have a mentor.

A mentor is your guide—the person to whom you look for good advice and practical wisdom. He or she is someone who is farther along the path than you and helps you to make your way.

Maybe you've thought of a mentor only in terms of career and work. Someone older, maybe higher up the chain of command, who takes you under his or her wing and helps you to find success. The kind of mentor you need will help you with all areas of your life, not just your career. He or she is the person to whom you can turn for practical and reliable advice.

As with the confidant, perhaps you have confused your need for a mentor with your need for a lover. It's a common mistake that has led many of us to painful relationships. We expected our lover to be someone who could take care of us *and* direct us along the path of life *and* dispense wisdom when it was needed. It's a tall order—too big for any one person to fill, so we ended up destroying a relationship trying to get more out of it than it could possibly provide.

Even more than with the confidant relationship, the confusion between mentor and lover is disastrous. To begin with, the mentoring relationship is one of a power imbalance—one person is vulnerable and the other invulnerable. The mentor has a great deal of power, and when that is mixed with a romantic relationship, it creates a prescription for abuse.

The obvious examples of the pitfalls of mixing a mentoring relationship with a love relationship can be seen between a client and a therapist or a minister and a congregant. The minister and the therapist hold powerful mentoring positions.

The less obvious examples can be seen between couples in which one person is willing to completely subordinate his or her will to that of another person. What is often at work here is the need for a mentor run amok. The one person is looking for a surrogate parent, while the other is willing to play the dominant role. It isn't a relationship on equal footing, and the one who subordinates his or her will inevitably gets hurt.

These kinds of mentoring relationships often happen for people who had a dysfunctional relationship with their parents. Since they are accustomed to abusive relationships and power imbalances, they slip into mentoring relationships that mimic their relationship with their parents. Eventually, they play out the entire drama of their childhood once again with a surrogate parent, a mentoring lover with all of the power. Until they become aware of how they are recreating the pain of their childhood, they will spend much of their lives repeating the misery—stuck in an unresolved crisis of contact.

A true mentoring relationship is one in which the mentor plays the role of the gentle sage. The importance of that role will vary over your life, but you will never rid yourself of the need for it. No matter how experienced at life you are, or how old you live to be, you will always have a hunger for someone to help you navigate the uncharted waters of your present moment.

Lettie's mentor is Fredericka. They've never called their relationship a "mentoring relationship," but it definitely serves that role for Lettie. It happens that Fredericka is several years older than Lettie and they come from similar backgrounds. Lettie and Fredericka don't see each other all that often—maybe once every couple of months—but the relationship has lasted for over fifteen years. Whatever Lettie is dealing with in her life, she knows that she can turn to Fredericka for good advice.

So what does Fredericka get out of this relationship? We all have a need to nurture others, and the mentoring relationship is a perfect outlet for that need. You've won some difficult battles in your life, and it feels good to share the secrets of your successes with someone else, and perhaps help them avoid the same struggle—or at least calm their fears while they go through the same experiences. It feels really good and right to help someone else, and that's what motivates Fredericka to maintain the relationship with Lettie.

Lettie ultimately makes her own decisions in life. Fredericka doesn't control Lettie. The relationship is one of generous advice between a "master" and an "apprentice," and it enhances both of their lives. It validates Fredericka's life to share her experiences with Lettie, and it helps Lettie to know that someone else has been where she is now.

Mentoring relationships come in all forms. Yours may be with your rabbi, your counselor, your grandparents, or your next-door neighbor. It can be a formal relationship, as between a counselor and a client, or informal, as between neighbors. Different mentoring relationships will satisfy your need at different points along your journey.

The important point isn't what kind of mentoring relationship you have, but that you have a mentor at all. Think about it. Don't you long for someone to whom you can go for advice that you can trust?

There's one final but important point about mentoring relationships: They are adult forms of the parent-child relationship. As you matured, your need for mother and father changed dramatically. Ideally, you became an adult friend to your parents as you became an adult yourself. The need for a mentor springs out of this transition in life. You need a new form of parenting—an adult parent. Not someone to provide for you, protect you, punish you, or make decisions for you, but someone to lovingly advise and counsel you— leaving the decisions strictly up to your adult will. Someone who supports and respects the independence of your being.

Sometimes people think of their mentor as a "second mom" or a "second dad" (and for a few very lucky people, it is their real mom or dad!). I think that's a wonderful way to describe the best kind of mentor—he or she is a beloved person in your life who gives to you graciously out of his or her own experience of living. It's a chance to experience a healthy parent as an adult, something many of us truly crave.

Do you have a mentor? What can you do to develop/enhance your relationship with your mentor?

NO ONE KNOWS ME

The self-induced trance that prevents you from developing the three intimate relationships you need is called *isolation*. The isolation trance isn't about being alone, it's about not revealing your true feelings to those around you. You remain among the people of your life and, at the same time, you shut them out of your true self.

There is a considerable risk in developing an intimate relationship: The other person could get to know you intimately and then reject you. That's the hardest kind of rejection to bear.

It's one thing for people who don't really know you to reject you, but quite another for those who you've let see "the real you." Coworkers, bosses, acquaintances, neighbors, customers, employees, teachers—all of these people can reject you, and it hurts, but not nearly as much as it would if your husband, wife, child, best friend, or sibling rejected you. Those rejections cut deeply and hurt for a long time. Rejection within an intimate relationship is one of the most painful wounds your psyche can bear.

The simple, preventive solution to this potentially devastating problem is simple and straightforward: Don't allow anyone to get too close. Or, stop allowing an intimate who you fear may reject you to know you in the present moment. You stop sharing your deepest feelings, especially if they are complex or difficult for another person to hear. You adopt a façade of "everything is just fine" when in your heart you know it isn't. You start protecting other people from the feelings that are burning within you. Instead, you do what you think will keep the other person's affection.

This is the trance of isolation. You stop allowing the real you to surface. You tell yourself that what you feel doesn't matter enough to express it and that it is better to play a "role" than to give voice to your innermost thoughts and feelings.

You induce the trance by telling yourself that what you are doing is for the best. "Better to spare someone else's feelings than to give voice to my own," you tell yourself again and again. As time goes on, the trance gets deeper and the real you becomes increasingly more different from the shell you present to the world. Eventually, you come to feel that no one really knows you and that no one loves you.

And you're right. You haven't allowed anyone to really see inside you for years. You've given them false impressions, conjured up smiles and empty hugs. They couldn't possibly have a clue who you are. Or what you really feel.

Rather than risk rejection, you've lived in a trance of isolation. You pushed away all possibility of intimate relationships, fearing the worst. You are unrejected and alone—and you crave the contact that only an intimate relationship can bring.

It's time to break the trance of isolation. How? It's actually easier than you might realize.

Pick someone important to you and start being totally honest about your relationship. When you feel angry, say so. When you feel sad, say so. When you feel romantic—even sexy—say so! Let it all hang out.

Believe me, the sparks will fly. You'll feel like a new person and the other person with whom you've chosen to be completely honest will be flabbergasted. Maybe he or she will respond to you. Maybe not. But this much I can promise: You'll feel more alive than you've ever felt in your life. Go on—give it a try. Make your motto, "Say so!"

What you'll discover is that it feels so good to let the real "you" out of that dark closet that you won't mind so much if the other person rejects you. It's totally liberating and exhilarating to break the trance of isolation.

Let me tell you something important—rejection isn't the end of the world. So someone doesn't like you. So someone peers into your soul and doesn't like what he or she sees. What difference does it make? Not one bit. In fact, sometimes being true and honest to yourself is the very thing you need to do to be able to figure out which relationships in your life are worth fighting for, and which are not.

The joy of life comes from experiencing yourself to the fullest, and you can't do that unless you have the three essential intimate relationships. Why are you trying to fake a life with people who don't really know you? You'll feel like a new person when you stop carrying that burden.

> *Think about the people currently in your life. With whom will you be completely honest, without any reservation or secrets?*

UNNATURAL AGREEMENTS

Let's take a look at some of the unnatural agreements that have prevented you from developing one of the three essential intimate relationships.

1. My Image Is More Important Than the Truth of Me

This agreement is a strong one, and it is born out of the best of intentions. Chances are, you started keeping this agreement at a very young age.

Your need for love and approval was so strong that you couldn't risk rejection from meaningful people in your life, so instead of learning to just be yourself, you became what you imagined would win their love. Slowly, you abandoned your own dreams and idiosyncrasies for an image of yourself that seemed more palatable to others.

When you start keeping this agreement at a young age, you become extremely well practiced at it. It becomes an automatic response to anticipate what others would like you to be and then act it out.

Over time, the significant people in your life never really get to know who you are. Instead, they know an image you have created. When they discover that the "you" they think they know isn't the real you (and they *will* eventually discover this—no one can keep up the act all the time), they become disillusioned and distance themselves from you. It is a fundamental breach of trust and it is the enemy of meaningful relationships.

You can see how this agreement is a huge barrier to developing the confidant relationship. Since trust is an essential ingredient, the confidant relationship never forms. Other people may enjoy you on a superficial level, but they would never trust you with their confidences. It is essentially the difference between cocktail banter and meaningful sharing. The latter is strictly reserved for those we trust.

2. No One Outside the Family Should Know My Secrets

Many people, particularly those who grew up in less-than-nurturing family environments, hold this agreement. Since their home life was filled with dysfunction and painful secrets, they learned not to "air their dirty laundry" outside the family. It is often drilled into the minds of young children that talking to a non–family member about the intimate details of his or her life or family is synonymous with treason.

If you grew up in such an environment, you probably have a great deal of difficulty opening up to someone who isn't a family member. You may not trust your family, but you have internalized a strict rule of silence outside the family circle.

A few people are blessed to find a confidant within their family, but most are not. If you refuse to open up to others on the outside, then you prevent yourself from developing the much-needed confidant relationship. The truth is, a real confidant will be as close to you as, if not closer than, any family member could be.

Families that have a strong patriarch (that is, a strong father or grandfather) or matriarch (that is, a strong mother or grandmother) also tend to keep this agreement among themselves. In these families there is a sharp line of distinction between family and outsiders. Outsiders are never to be trusted with family matters—only other family members are trusted.

3. My Confidant, Lover, or Mentor Must Look, Act, and Be a Certain Kind of Person

Susan, a good friend of mine, was recently complaining about a male friend, David, who was in her life. David was extremely kind and caring of Susan although the two of them were not romantically involved (and had no intention of becoming involved), and his attention toward her seemed to bother Susan. "Why doesn't he find himself a girlfriend?" Susan said. "It just doesn't seem right that he is so attentive to me."

When Susan finished, a mutual acquaintance of ours who was hearing this said something extremely profound: "Isn't it strange how wonderful people come into our lives, *and it isn't enough?"* We were all silent for a moment as we digested that morsel of wisdom. Sometimes the perfect confidant lands in our lap, but we don't see it because we are intentionally or unintentionally looking for a lover.

What Susan said is true of many people caught in the contact crisis. They have a preconceived notion of what their lover, confidant, and mentor should be. If the package doesn't fit, then they never allow themselves to pursue the relationship. As a result, they miss out on many fulfilling and loving relationships with people who don't fit their carefully constructed scenario. Wonderful people come our way, but we are so blinded by our expectations that we can't see how truly wonderful they are. By keeping this agreement, we are the ones who lose out.

4. It's Better Not to Burden Someone Else With My Troubles

"Why would someone else want to know the details of my life?" You may have learned as a child that other people aren't interested in hearing about the intimate details of your life, so you avoid such conversations. You keep it light and friendly because that's what you believe other people want from you.

What this agreement denies is that by sharing your life story with someone, you actually have something of value to offer him or her. Your life lessons are meaningful, not only to you, but to others who are close to you. By sharing what you've suffered and how you've learned from that suffering, you help your confidant discover new perspectives on his or her own life.

This agreement prevents you from experiencing the deeper satisfaction that comes from two people sharing their souls with each other, flaws and all. When you keep the relationship "light and friendly," you can't experience the fullness of each other. Not until you are willing to trust someone enough to tell him or her the whole truth about yourself will you find the confidant relationship you crave.

5. Others Will Eventually Betray the Secrets I Have Told Them

This agreement is a big one for those who have experienced painful betrayal in their lives. I once worked with a client whose husband had run off with her best friend. She felt utterly betrayed by her friend, whom she thought she knew. For years after that, she had difficulty trusting anyone, male or female. Only when she acknowledged this agreement was she able to allow herself to trust others enough to find the companionship she so needed and missed.

If you are unwilling to risk betrayal, you will never experience real love. If you are unwilling to reveal the contents of your soul to another person, you will never know the joy of complete companionship.

Businesswoman and lecturer Annette Simmons often says, "Resentment keeps the wrong person up at night." Likewise, bitterness and regret over a past betrayal will only prevent you from trusting and creating the mutually satisfying relationships you need.

> *What unnatural agreements have kept you from discovering your lover, confidant, and mentor?*

FINDING EMOTIONAL CONTACT

Resolving your crisis of contact happens when you experience the truth that you must trust other people in order to be happy and fulfilled. No matter what has happened to you at the hands of others, your ultimate happiness demands that you trust despite your fear.

As long as you are unwilling to make yourself vulnerable to another person, you will remain in crisis. You will grow lonely and alienated, angry at a world that you cannot trust. Happiness in life never occurs in isolation. Until you begin to trust someone outside yourself, you remain in crisis.

The Four Stages of the Crisis of Contact

1. Breaking the trance of isolation

You create a trance of isolation—distancing yourself from others—so that you don't have to reveal your true self.

2. Confronting the crisis

You acknowledge that your relationships are, for the most part, emotionally dishonest.

3. Sorting through the confusion

You begin removing the façade that you've presented to the world and revealing your true feelings. Sometimes both you and others are confused by the change. They ask, "Who are you?"

4. Resolving the crisis

You begin to trust others enough to always reveal your true self to them, regardless of how you imagine they will react.

Why Can't I Believe in Myself?

[THE CRISIS OF SELF-CONFIDENCE]

There is one simple question that makes all the difference between self-confidence and self-doubt, between a life of success and one of mostly failures. It is a question you've heard before, and maybe you've even asked it of yourself. The amazing power of this question lies in the degree of honesty with which you answer it. This question is: "What is your talent?"

Knowing your strengths and abilities is the key to understanding and resolving the crisis of self-confidence. Until you know your talents, you don't truly know yourself. How can you have confidence in something that remains a mystery to you?

Go ahead, ask yourself: What are my talents? Take a few minutes to write what you think are five of your talents. These can be anything from your ability to calculate complex mathematical equations to your gift for interacting with children, from your magnificent singing voice to your flair for organizing large groups of people.

Could you do this exercise with ease? Did you think about it for some time before you could answer the question? How confident are you that this list is an accurate assessment of your strengths?

Look at your list and beside each talent put a rating, from 1 to 5, indicating how confident you are that is one of your talents, with "1" being "not at all confident" and "5" being "highly confident."

How confident were you in your list? Are most of your ratings somewhere around 3 or lower? If so, you are facing a crisis in self-confidence.

A clear, unwavering knowledge of your talent is the cornerstone of self-confidence. Until you really know your talents and what they can do, you can't believe in yourself and your potential.

Without self-confidence, real success in life will always elude you.

Why is this? Success comes only from the natural blossoming of your individual, idiosyncratic talent. When you allow yourself to discover and develop that talent, you grow into the path that is meant for you. That path may be dramatically different from all other paths, but it is right for you and will bring you your greatest successes. It is the only path to achieving your best.

And despite your most treasured fantasies of becoming something different, greater, smarter, or more talented, you cannot escape your innate abilities. What makes some people truly great at what they do is a confident reliance on their particular strengths. So it is with you: What will make you successful is not imitating someone else's success, but realizing your own potential.

Once you grasp this, you will be on your way to achieving your highest potential. Success lies not in acquiring something outside yourself or being something else, but in *maximizing* the talent you already have.

You are a portfolio of talents. This portfolio (which is within you at this very moment) is all you will ever have. Your challenge lies in leveraging those talents maximally. You don't need to "get something" for success. You don't need to emulate someone else. All you need you already own.

Think of your talent as the DNA of your destiny. Talent is the sacred seed of the life you are meant to have—the one you truly desire. It is your choice whether you will trust these seeds and allow them to grow. You, and you alone, choose whether you will have complete fulfillment by following those talents.

TALENT IS THE GOLDEN KEY

The research on the highest achievers in all areas of life is clear. The one thread—the only thread—that connects all of those who have sustained successful, productive lives is that they relied heavily upon their strengths. They didn't waste time in jobs that didn't tap their strongest talents. Nor did they waste time trying to be good at something of which they weren't capable. Instead, they created a life in which they could practice their talents, allowing them to achieve great things in life.

There's something else you should know about your talent: Those people who discover their talent and focus on it are more fulfilled in life than those who don't. Even though their lives are just as hectic, demanding, frustrating, challenging, and physically tiring as all the rest, they find themselves rejuvenated by doing their jobs. Instead of ending the day exhausted and mentally depleted, they fall asleep tired but content at having engaged their talents. They are mentally, emotionally, and spiritually energized by their life.

Life is full of temptation to abandon your personal talents. The next, better promotion at work isn't exactly what is motivating and challenges you most, but it does offer a great salary, more corporate exposure, and a better title. And so does the next position. Within a few years, it is easy to find yourself in a job that has little meaning for you and doesn't really tap your best abilities. If you choose to allow it, you can be promoted into your highest level of incompetence.

So what restrains you? What holds you back from trusting and maximizing your talents? You induce the trance of *low self-esteem*. You tell yourself that you are inadequate for the challenges that face you each day. You tell yourself that you must be something more than what you are. You tell yourself that your gifts are not sufficient to create the life you want. Over and over again you focus your mind on these suggestions until you perpetually live in a trance of low self-esteem.

Why Can't I Believe in Myself?

Why a trance of low self-esteem? Simply put, it lets you off the hook. As long as you tell yourself that you don't have any talent or special ability, you don't have to hold yourself responsible for not discovering those talents and using them. Who can blame you for not using something that you don't have? It's easier to *believe* that you have no talent than to do the difficult work of discovering, developing, and trusting your talents.

As long as you live in the trance of low self-esteem, you have the perfect excuse for living an unremarkable life. It is far more painful, indeed, to look back on your life and think that you squandered a great gift than it would be to imagine you never had the gift in the first place. By living in the trance of low self-esteem, you live with the fantasy that you have no gifts.

By living in this trance, you steal from yourself the success that is your birthright. To resolve the crisis of self-confidence, your first challenge is to break the trance, and to begin the work of discovering your talent.

How have you used the trance of low self-esteem to avoid making the most of your gifts?

THE CRUCIBLE OF TALENT

Talent is an intrinsic potential that was given to you at birth. At the point that you are reading this book, you already have your lifelong talents. What you do best is already determined, and should you choose to use your talents, you will realize this vast potential. What you become in life starts with talent and manifests itself with *what you do with that talent*. Any job or relationship—anything that prevents you from developing your unique talents—diminishes both your ultimate fulfillment and achievement. It blocks you from being your best.

No one is without talent and plenty of it. Everyone does some things better than others. Everyone has some glowing strengths that, if given the chance, can outshine his or her weaknesses.

Of course, this isn't to say that you can be the very best at *everything* you do. You may get great pleasure and satisfaction out of running although you could never compete in the Olympics. You may have a fabulous sense of economics, perfectly suited to your career, although you would not be able to do Alan Greenspan's job. But that doesn't mean you should stop running or should change professions. Talent in a given area allows you to achieve a great deal while doing your personal best. It has nothing to do with perfection.

To begin understanding what talent is, there are two other things you need to understand: They are *advantages* and *experience*. Both of these things are often wrongly confused with talent. So that you don't make that mistake, let's take a quick look at them.

ADVANTAGES

Advantages are things that give us an extra boost in life, such as a great education, wealth, high intelligence, or a charming personality. As helpful as these gifts can be, advantages only *augment* talent—they can never substitute for it.

Advantages are often confused with talent—especially in job interviews and other places where you must rely on a written résumé to summarize your abilities. In fact, the writing of a résumé is inherently biased toward advantages because they are easily written down. Things like degrees, certificates, extracurricular activities, fellowships, and great references can be easily and succinctly written down. Talent, on the other hand, is very hard to describe in words, at least in a convincing manner. Many people often make the mistake of interpreting advantages as signs of talent when, in fact, they aren't. Some of the most well-written résumés that are chock full of advantages come from people who have yet to discover their real talent.

One of the best examples of how the advantage of education isn't a good substitute for talent comes from the extremely well-respected head of the Federal Reserve System, Alan Greenspan. Unless you were told, you might never guess where this financial genius's degree comes from: Juilliard School of Music. Not exactly the place where you would expect to discover one of the most respected financial leaders of our time! The point to remember is that education can be a wonderful advantage, but it is not a reliable substitute for talent. In all probability, Alan Greenspan would never have attained the level of success he has enjoyed had he pursued music as his career.

As with education, high intelligence is not a talent but an advantage. Simply being "bright" doesn't guarantee that you can do whatever you decide to do well. Having the intelligence to do something doesn't mean you will choose to do it, or that you will succeed at it.

In 1921, the famous Stanford University psychologist Lewis Terman started a study of the impact of intelligence on lifelong outcomes. The study began with 1,470 genius-level children and followed them throughout their lifetimes. Since the lifespan of these children exceeded the career of Terman, he transferred the study to Drs. Robert and Pauline Sears upon his retirement. After nearly a half-century of study, the Searses published their results. What distinguished spectacular achievement from low achievement or failure among the study participants was "prudence and forethought, willpower, perseverance and desire. They chose among their talents and concentrated their efforts." Those children, now well into their senior years, revealed that intelligence alone is not enough to guarantee success. Those who succeeded did so by persistently relying on their talent.

EXPERIENCE

Talent is often confused with experience, too. That you have done a job or a task for many years does not mean that you are good at the job or even capable of being good at it. For example, I might spend my entire career as an advertising copywriter, acquire all the knowledge of the field, and still not be very good at writing advertising copy.

Like education, talent thrives on experience. The person with a talent for a particular task gets better with practice and experience. As his or her experience increases, the potential of talent becomes a reality. Experience refines and develops your talent, but experience at a job for which you have little talent produces consistently mediocre results, little personal growth, and worst of all, prevents you from spending the same precious time and energy growing and succeeding in the area of your talents.

Now that we've explored what talent is and how it is different from advantages and experience, we're ready to dive in and discover our own talents.

What are your advantages? What experiences do you have that make you competent today? How might you have confused these two things with your talent?

DISCOVERING YOUR TALENT

"If only I had some talent." I hear this all the time from well-meaning people who have no self-confidence. "I can't do anything *special*," they tell me.

I must disagree with their perception of themselves. Everyone has talent. Each person has certain strengths and interests that, while they may lie dormant, are contained within the self. There is overwhelming evidence to suggest that persons of every imaginable background, socioeconomic status, education, and personality profile have unique talents.

The birthing of a talent is an uncontrollable, natural process. While we cannot force it, there are several common hallmarks of an emerging talent. Let's take a look at three of them.

YEARNINGS

The first hallmark of talent is a *yearning*. A yearning is a pull toward some activity and is most often felt after we watch someone else engaged in that activity. It is a heartfelt magnetism that tugs at us and urges us to action.

Bruce Hangen, conductor of the Omaha Symphony Orchestra, describes one of his earliest yearnings to be a conductor: "Just sitting there in my position as first cellist, I knew I wanted to get up and lead the orchestra, and I knew I could do it better than my teacher."[1] Shortly thereafter, Hangen's junior-high music teacher handed him the baton, and his career as a conductor was launched.

Another prominent example of a yearning happened to a young Fred Smith while attending Yale. During his junior year, Smith wrote a paper that described a hub-and-spokes system of overnight freight forwarding. Smith was mesmerized by the possibilities of such an efficient system, which he imagined could be composed of both airline and truck routes. Despite the incredible cost of creating such a national system, which would need to be fully operational on the first day of operation, Smith persisted with the idea after graduation. Numerous experts and business analysts pronounced his idea impractical (starting with his Yale professor, who gave the paper a grade of "C" on the basis of feasibility), but Smith strove on, eventually raising $72 million in investment capital, which started the company now known as Federal Express.

On March 12, 1973, Federal Express opened for business, sending its airplanes from all over the country (the "spokes") to Memphis (the "hub") to deliver an underwhelming total of six packages. After losing millions of dollars over the next few years, Federal Express eventually became profitable and evolved into the world's premier overnight delivery service—all starting from the yearning of a college student.

It is very important to state, however, that yearnings aren't sufficient to indicate talent. Certainly, everyone has had the experience of wanting to do something for which they weren't suited: write the great American novel, sing at the

Metropolitan Opera, or cook a gourmet meal. These yearnings are generally fantasies that are based on fame, glamour, or excitement.

A great example of misleading yearnings based on glamour is a study conducted by SRI Gallup on flight attendants for a major airline. What the study found was that flight attendants who were enticed into the profession by the glamorous fantasy of travel to exotic locations tended to have poor performance records and short-lived careers (eighteen months or less). Those who became flight attendants because they enjoyed making other people comfortable were highly rated and tended to have a long-term career with the airline.

How do you know if a yearning to do something is a pointer to your talent? Ask yourself, "Have I experienced any success doing this?" If you yearn to be an opera singer, have you experienced any success with music or singing? If you yearn to be a writer, have you experienced any success in writing? If you yearn to be a chef, have you had any successes in the kitchen? If the answer is yes, then your yearning is pointing you in the direction of your talent.

Remember the story about Jeannie? She opened her dream dress shop, but after a year it failed. Why? While she definitely had a yearning to own a shop, she unfortunately didn't also have the talent for running a small business. A yearning by itself isn't enough, but the yearnings worth paying attention to will lead you to your true talents.

Yearnings, while not sufficient to indicate talent, always surround talent. You tend to be naturally drawn to do those

things for which you have the potential for excellence.
Yearnings are one of nature's pointers to your highest good.

*What have you yearned to do in life? Have you acted
on that yearning?*

SATISFACTION

Another hallmark of talent is satisfaction. When you
engage in activities for which you have talent, it feels good,
especially when you notice that your skill is improving with
practice. There is a strong feeling of contentment, a sense that
you are doing something that is meaningful.

Once, while working with a national retailer, I encountered two district managers who, although they covered different territories, had identical jobs. Both had equally experienced store managers reporting to them and their sales
numbers were roughly equivalent. One of the managers, Tom,
had been a district manager for most of his career. Tom had
worked for several national companies, and, as with most district managers, had spent much of his life traveling from one
store to the next. Tom was in his early fifties and despite his
age, kept up a grueling travel schedule. Tom was well respected

within the company and was often used as a mentor for new district managers who were sent to learn from him.

Judy was the other district manager. Judy had been a district manager for more than a decade and was very ambitious. Unfortunately, Judy didn't have much talent for working with people, and her relationships with her store managers suffered badly as a result. I traveled with Judy for several days, visiting many of her stores with her. Each time we entered a store, I could see the dread on the faces of the store and department managers.

The differences between Tom and Judy were profound. No matter how hectic his schedule, Tom appeared rested and alert. He was attentive to the people around him and made them feel comfortable in his presence. Judy, on the other hand, always seemed stressed and a bit tired. She worked hard, but didn't seem to enjoy her job.

Over several years, I worked with Judy in therapy. In time, she admitted that she really disliked her job, but since she had worked so hard to get her position, she was hesitant to let it go. Besides, she wasn't sure that she could make as much money doing something else. Eventually, the stress of trying to succeed in a position for which she wasn't suited wore her down and she quit.

Despite the fact that Tom was twenty years older than Judy, he continued to thrive in his position. The pressures of the job seemed to challenge him to do his best, and he handled them with grace and exuberance. Tom found great satisfaction in his job and couldn't imagine himself doing anything else.

The difference between Tom and Judy is in the satisfaction that talent brings. Tom found nourishment for his heart and mind through his work. Judy found herself drained and depleted. When you engage your talents, you will find yourself in the position of Tom: No matter how great the pressure—even when you are physically tired by it—you will find contentment and challenge in your work and in your life.

What two or three things give you satisfaction? How can you do them more often?

RAPID LEARNING

Another very reliable and important hallmark of talent is *rapid learning.* Where your talent leads you, you go more quickly. Even though you may never have tried your hand at the task, it feels as if you have done it before. Your innate ability assimilates you to the experience with ease, and you quickly gain finesse.

The phenomenon of rapid learning is something we have all experienced in ourselves or in others. Immediately we recognize this as the beginning of talent: "She's a natural." "He has found his niche." "She's got the knack for it."

Slow learning, on the other hand, is a good indicator of the absence of talent. No matter how strong the yearning to do something, if we find that our progress is frustrating and slow, it's most likely not one of our talents.

The clearest example of rapid learning in my own life came from my teenage years when I learned to play the piano. My piano teacher, a very qualified concert pianist, struggled for years teaching me to read and play classical music. I, a willing but slow student, spent hours trying to master the works of great composers, but found that I progressed very slowly in my ability to read both the notes and timing of the more complex piano music. Year after year went by while I labored at trying to improve my reading skills with very little progress. I was definitely a slow learner.

On the weekends, however, I had great fun playing the piano and organ at the church my family attended. Since I knew many of the old hymns from early childhood, I found I could sit down and play them without music. Much to the horror of my piano teacher (who attended the same church), I stopped reading music and played solely by ear. If my piano teacher would play a piece of music for me first, I could cover up my weak reading skills by imitating what I had heard. Eventually, my music teacher and I agreed that teaching me to read music was not worthwhile, and I quit the lessons. To this day, I still play the piano almost entirely by ear.

Clearly, my talent was not in reading or playing classical music, but in imitating notes that I heard. Playing by ear was not a struggle for me. In fact, I often felt that I was "cheating" when I opted to play what I heard instead of the sheet music I couldn't read. My rapid, effortless learning to play by ear was a good sign of where my musical talents lay.

> *Think back over your life. What things have you seemed to learn more quickly than others?*

Yearnings, satisfaction, and rapid learning are all good indications of talent. When all three are present, you can be certain that you have a natural ability to do the task at hand. While none of these things guarantees that you will be the best, they do indicate that you have found the niche *that is the best for you.*

To help you get clear on your talent, complete the following exercise:

What things do you yearn to do?	What things have you learned to do quickly in your life?	What activities bring you satisfaction?

Now, look over the chart you just completed. List the themes that emerge as you scan all three columns. For example, you might notice that themes such as "organizing things and people" or "helping others to be their best" or "researching the facts" run through all three columns. Whatever themes emerge, however surprising they may seem to you now, write them down here:

1. _____

2. _____

3. _____

4. _____

5. _____

These themes represent your talent. They are descriptions of innate abilities you have that enable you to do things well.

STOP TRYING TO FIX YOURSELF

So many people, eager to become their best, try to do so by improving their weaknesses. They read books, they attend seminars, and they try, try, try. But try as they may, they rarely improve. Those who don't have strong "people skills" rarely improve their skills by taking the "managing relationships" or "dealing with difficult people" seminar. Those who have difficulty managing their time rarely improve by purchasing an expensive daily planner or sophisticated time-management software. This is a very important insight: You won't improve through remedial education directed at your weaknesses. *You improve by unleashing the power of your strengths.*

In other words, focus on what you do well, and practice, practice, practice. When you engage your strengths, you invariably refine and improve. Then, any problems created by your weaknesses automatically diminish. You don't fix your weaknesses—you escape them through your strengths.

Time and again, I've found this to be true in my life. I am a capable psychologist and writer, but a terrible salesman. When I practice being a psychologist or a writer, I become better at those tasks, and despite years of trying to improve my sales skills (and lots of personal flagellation), I haven't improved much at all. What I have discovered, however, is that the more I work with clients, the more knowledge and experience I gain for future clients, and the more I write, the better my writing becomes. As I practice these strengths, my clients recommend me to new clients and my books attract more readers, consequently diminishing my need to constantly promote myself. My work has become my career sales tool. My strengths have overcome my weaknesses.

This is NOT the same thing as sweeping your weaknesses under the rug of denial. Rather, it is the process of acknowledging and befriending those weaknesses. *Be very clear about your shortcomings. If you don't know them, you can't know your strengths either.* When you know what you do well, you must in the same thought know what you don't do well.

So how do you get to know your true weaknesses? Some of your weaknesses are probably already apparent to you—every time you do a certain thing, you seem to fail. Other weaknesses you may not see that easily. To discover these, think back over your recent history about the times you've become frustrated and disappointed. Take a minute and list ten instances you can remember.

Now look at your list. Is there a theme, a certain thing you do that always seems to precede frustration and disappointment? For example, you might notice that you continually fail when you start to feel particularly stressed, or when you are forced to confront another person. Bingo—these themes are most likely pointing to one of your weaknesses. Repeated frustration in similar situations is almost always the product of one of your weaknesses.

Stop trying to fix yourself. Instead, befriend your weaknesses and do what is necessary to manage them, or surround yourself with others who can compensate for them. *But spend your time and energy on your strengths.* As you do, your talents will far outweigh the weaknesses that may now seem insurmountable.

TALENT ENVY

When you focus on your weaknesses instead of on your strengths, you waste precious time and energy trying to do something for which you are not suited. Rather than building on your strengths, you idolize the strengths of others and wish for yourself talent you do not possess. You may imitate your heroes, but you will never equal their performance, because they, not you, have the talent for that particular activity. The more attention you give to acquiring someone else's talent, the less you give to the talent you do have.

"Talent envy" is utterly self-defeating. When you find yourself continually ill equipped to handle a situation, it is the *situation* that must be changed, not you. Success demands that you place yourself in situations that employ your strengths. To remain in an over-challenging job, trying to convince yourself that you are invincible, that you can handle whatever is thrown at you, is very foolish. The great opera diva Maria Callas would never have succeeded as a pop singer. The golfing champion Tiger Woods would have failed as a football linebacker. And you will never reach your greatest accomplishments by dwelling on improving your weaknesses. Be consumed with what you do well, not what you wish you did well, or worse, what you cannot do.

RUST-OUT

Another way in which people fail to fulfill their talents is through nonuse. They "tread water" in jobs and relationships that don't allow them to really excel, hoping that "good enough" will do the job.

For these people, their talents become rusty or remain undeveloped. Instead, they become minimally competent at fulfilling the expectations of others. It isn't their "strong suit," but it is what they believe is required of them. They never excel, but they don't fail, either. Rather than maximizing their strongest talents, they try to be what they think other people expect, and since they aren't using their innate potential, they do little more than get by. Their unused abilities lie dormant, and their lives suffer from talent "rust-out."

What is so tragic about this scenario is that each of us has far more potential than we will likely tap in our lifetime. When you ignore that potential, you settle for less success than you could otherwise achieve.

Your success lies within your talents. There is no other way to reach your highest potential for success.

Take, for example, pro golfer Brad Faxon. In 1984, Faxon finished 124th on the money list and barely held on to his PGA card. While it was generally acknowledged that Faxon's strong suit was his skill with a wedge and a putter, he was spending most of his time trying to improve the weaker aspects of his game—to hit the ball straighter and to cultivate more power in his swing. That's when noted sports psychologist Bob Rotella was able to convince Faxon that his focus was misplaced. He encouraged Faxon to concentrate on the strengths of his game. "You don't have to be the best driver in the world," Rotella recalls telling him, "because you've got a great short game and a great mind."

Taking Rotella's advice to heart, Faxon focused on his

putting game and became even better around the greens, to the point where many consider him the best putter on the PGA tour. As a result, he has earned a place on two Ryder Cup teams and, remarkably, he finished eighth on the money list in 1996. Rotella sums up Faxon's success: "He's really learned to love his game and not wish he had somebody else's."[2]

YOU CAN'T HAVE IT ALL

I really hate to share the news, but it's true: you can't have it all. You're not destined to have it all. You can't be anything you wish to be simply because you put your mind to it. Life doesn't work that way, and despite the crates of self-help books trying to sell that bill of goods, it's just not the truth. Instead, you are programmed for a particular kind of success. Your talents predispose you to do certain things well, other things decently, and still others not at all. They define for you the path you are meant to tread.

The belief that "I can do anything if I just believe it and try hard enough" has ruined more lives than almost anything else. These people try and try, butting their heads against rock-solid walls, failing to accomplish anything productive but failing to give up.

These well-meaning people remind me of my pet English bulldog, Winston. Winston loves nothing more than a good game of tug-of-war, and he will hold on to his end of the rope, no matter what. Even when he has been so overpowered that his playful opponent pulls him off the floor, he sets his teeth into the rope, dangling in midair. His tenacity is endearing, but the truth is, it isn't very productive. Likewise, heroic persistence in the face of likely defeat may make for great action-hero myths, but in reality it isn't fruitful. Some battles we were never meant to fight, much less win, and no amount of positive thinking and persistence will change this.

THE BUSINESS OF TALENT

When you practice your talents, the world beats a path to your door. When you give what you have to give and speak your truth, you fulfill your purpose in this world. The author Arnold Patent said it well: "If you have a genuine need to say something, someone has a genuine need to hear it."

You err dramatically when you first try to figure out what the world wants from you, and then attempt to give that gift. If the world already knew what it needed from you, then what need would there be for you and all your uniqueness? Are you nothing more than a cosmic mule whose only function is to kowtow to the dictates of your environment? Are you simply an interchangeable cog in a giant machine?

Of course not. The truth is, the world doesn't know what you should say. It doesn't know what gift you should give.

Why? Because you haven't yet given it. You have something unique and precious to give. The giving of that gift in one stroke creates a need and a solution. This is the circle of life: You give your talents to the world and the world responds by giving you what you need to prosper.

The evidence of the overwhelming power of our talents is everywhere. We didn't know we needed light bulbs until Thomas Edison gave from his talents. We didn't know how inspiring water lilies could be until Claude Monet painted them. We didn't know how poorly the mentally ill were treated until Dorothea Dix showed the world with her detailed reports and demonstrations. We didn't know how computers could change our personal lives until Steve Wozniac (cofounder, Apple Computers) showed us. Americans didn't need a precious symbol of liberty until the French gave us the Statue of Liberty, and now we can't imagine New York City harbor without it.

So why is it that so many of us fail to focus upon and maximize our innate talents and consequently, never really succeed? Why do we try to have it all instead of trying to do that which we are capable of? Why is it that we are unable to completely trust the reservoir of ability inside ourselves and instead waste time trying to do tasks for which we have no potential for success? If we have within ourselves everything we need to reach our highest achievements and fulfillment, why do we settle for something less?

The answer is simple enough: We fail to know our talents. Learn the lesson now. Focus on your talent, and only on your talent. In the end, it will lead you to your destiny.

How have you focused on your shortcomings rather than your talent? What are your talents? How can you practice your talents more often?

This is truth that will resolve your crisis: Know your talents. You will never be self-assured until you know that you can trust your own strengths. As long as you focus on everything else—including your weaknesses—you will never have the self-confidence you crave. Discover, know, practice, fight for, honor, and invest in your talents.

The Four Stages of the Crisis of Self-Confidence

1. Breaking the trance of low self-esteem

You create a trance of low self-esteem—feeling as if you aren't very capable at anything—to avoid holding yourself responsible for not using your talent.

2. Confronting the crisis

You acknowledge that you don't really know what your talents are.

3. Sorting through the confusion

You begin to explore different kinds of activities until you discover what you do well.

4. Resolving the crisis

You learn what your strengths are and how to rely on them to make yourself successful.

How Can I Become My Own Person?

[The Crisis of Individuation]

Undoubtedly one of the scariest days you will experience is the day when you, as an adult, make a major life decision that you know your parents will disagree with. It brings up feelings of abandonment that can be completely overwhelming. In fact, they may be so overwhelming that you abandon your decision and do instead what you think will keep the approval of your parents.

This is the crisis of individuation and it is a powerful force in your life. Separating yourself from your parents' hopes, dreams, and values is a major turning point in life. Finding the courage to become an individual (to *individuate*) is a process that can take years. It wouldn't be unusual if you were well into your adult life before you truly resolve this crisis and individuate. Some people never do.

The love and attention of your parents has been tremendously important to you and has sustained you through both good and hard times. When you failed at school or lost your best friend, their love helped you to get through the pain. In times of need or sorrow, you turned to them because you could rely on their love.

Even with their flaws and inability to love you completely and unconditionally, you relied on the love they were able to give. It was your emotional lifeline.

When the day comes that your own dreams for the future clash with what you know your parents wish for you, you must make a choice: "Do I follow my parents' wishes or do I follow my own?"

For many of us, early life decisions are made with our parents' wishes honored in some way. We may not do exactly what they wish, but we compromise in a way that we think will not drive them from us and at the same time give us what we want.

As a result, those early life decisions may not have been good for you. Why? Because they were a compromise that doesn't fully satisfy you or your parents.

Kathryn's parents live in Miami, Florida, where they have lived all their lives. When Kathryn became an adult, they often mentioned how they hoped that Kathryn would live near them so that when the grandchildren were born, they could be nearby and close to their grandchildren.

Kathryn, however, really wanted to live in San Francisco, where she went to college and where she met her husband. Afraid to disappoint her parents, she and her husband settled in Orlando, Florida, so that they could be a short plane flight away from her parents. It was a complex decision that didn't satisfy Kathryn, her husband, or Kathryn's parents. It was a compromise that Kathryn had erroneously imagined would be accepted better by her parents, since it kept her in the state of Florida.

As you might imagine, Kathryn was miserable living in Orlando and her parents complained bitterly about not seeing the grandkids often enough.

Like Kathryn, you probably made early adult decisions that didn't satisfy you, but you thought would be acceptable to your parents. Perhaps it was your major in college, where you worked, who you married, or where you bought your first house.

The question you must ask yourself now is, "Am I still making compromise decisions about my life?" When you think about changing jobs, where your children will go to school, or within what religion they will be raised, do you make such decisions with your parents' approval in mind? If you do, then individuation is a crisis you must resolve.

Sarah rebelled against her parents during high school. She dated boys whom she knew her parents wouldn't approve of, went to a college in Chicago against their wishes, and eventually married a man who was divorced and had two children. Her parents, devout Catholics, were critical of Sarah's choices and let her know it frequently through subtle and not-so-subtle remarks about her life.

Despite the fact that Sarah had gone against her parents' wishes, she had done so without resolving her crisis of individuation. She was upset and angry with her parents for not approving of her choices.

By the time Sarah had two children, she began doing things she said she never would do: She raised her children in Catholic school and began insisting that she and her family spend every vacation visiting her parents in Phoenix, Arizona. Over the years, Sarah began to look and act just like her parents, making choices for herself and her family that she knew they would approve of.

By the time Sarah was in her mid-forties, she was often depressed. Her life had not turned out as she imagined, and although she had done "all the right things," she wasn't happy at all. Her husband complained that she was nothing like the woman he married and eventually asked her for a divorce.

Now, a single mother with two teenage children, Sarah took a job that didn't really interest her but paid the bills. She felt as if her life was totally ruined.

Sarah was plagued by a crisis of individuation that she hadn't ever resolved. Although she started out trying to separate from her parents emotionally, the imagined terror of their disapproval drove her back into the role of the dutiful daughter. Her life became an enactment of their wishes rather than a blossoming of Sarah.

The problem was, Sarah didn't really know what she wanted in life. She had spent so many years under the influence of her parents' dreams and values that she hadn't allowed her own to emerge.

If you are in the beginning stages of individuation, you might not know what you want out of life either. Because you have slowed the development of your own dreams and values by following your parents', your dreams haven't fully emerged into your awareness. You may be an adult, but at this point psychologically you're still a child.

That may be hard for you to hear, and I can certainly understand why. No adult likes to think of himself or herself as a child. It can be very disturbing to realize that you've never really grown up.

But this is a fact you must face. If you find yourself subjecting your will to that of your parents on a regular basis, if you defer to your parents on major life decisions, or if you find that you have accepted many of your values and beliefs because "that's the way you were raised," then you haven't individuated. Emotionally you're still connected to your parents, much as a child is emotionally dependent upon his or her mother.

Let's pause for a moment and deal with a question I know you've wanted to ask. "What's wrong with wanting to please my parents?"

Nothing. Absolutely nothing. The problem isn't in pleasing your parents: It is that you want to please your parents to the point of sacrificing yourself. For fear that they might reject you if you were different from them, you avoided developing into your own individual self.

You've got to accept one hard fact: *You are different from your parents.* You are an individual with needs, wants, desires, dreams, and values that are uniquely yours. Some of these things you will naturally share with your parents. Some you will not.

You aren't a bad person because you aren't a carbon copy of your parents. You aren't being disrespectful of your parents because you chose to develop fully into your own self. In fact, you can never really love your parents until you allow yourself to grow up emotionally and see them as individuals like yourself, doing the best they know how.

As you probably already know, deferring to your parents creates within you a strong feeling of resentment. Why? Because somewhere deep inside you, you know that you are dependent upon them and that you are sacrificing your own life to earn their approval—and that hurts. You can't possibly have the loving, supportive relationship you've always wanted with that kind of resentment stirring inside you.

It's also important to know that reacting *against* your parents isn't individuation. Children who spend their lives in rebellion against their parents aren't individuated; they are merely reacting to their parents. Even though they're no longer trying to please their parents, their parents' wishes are still controlling them, even if it is in reverse fashion. As long as your parents are a central factor in your life decisions (whether a positive or a negative one), you haven't resolved the crisis of individuation.

An unresolved crisis of individuation ultimately deteriorates your relationship with your parents. You resent the control they wield over your life and begin to dislike the part of you that gives them control. Your relationship with them becomes colored with these strong, negative emotions that spill out in all sorts of ways. Visiting with your parents begins to feel more like an obligation and less like a pleasant opportunity, and the relationship becomes less and less loving and enjoyable as time passes. In the end, by not resolving the crisis of individuation and creating a life of your own, you destroy the very relationship you have been trying so hard to preserve.

When you successfully resolve your crisis of individuation, you no longer yearn for the approval of your parents. When they disapprove of what you do, it isn't pleasant, but it doesn't stir within you those childhood fears of abandonment and rejection. You begin to see your parents in a new way—as flawed individuals like yourself who are trying to do the best they can with what they know. Maybe it isn't the best way, or even the healthiest way, but they are doing what they know how to do. You can enjoy them as friends if they are willing, or at the very least as fellow adults. The resentment of broken childhood dreams begins to fade when you successfully individuate and you can honestly forgive your parents for their shortcomings. You see them not as ruthless gatekeepers of the love you need, but rather as fellow human beings who are trying to live a loving and happy life to the best of their ability.

You're far better off following your own passions and values than trying to acquiesce to the dictates of your parents'. If there is to be a fulfilling relationship, it must be based on mutual trust and respect. Nothing less is worth having.

There are several unnatural agreements that keep you from individuating. Here are some of the more common.

1. I Must Live My Parents' Unlived Dream

Most parents have grand dreams for their children. In their own way, they want the best life has to offer for their children. However well-meaning those dreams may be, they often weigh heavily upon a child, and can actually hurt the child as he or she grows up. How? When a child (particularly a grown child) refuses to follow his or her own passion and, instead, tries to fulfill his or her parents' expectations.

Many of life's major decisions, including your choice of career, your marriage partner, where you live, how much you travel, and how many children you have, can be heavily influenced by your parents' expectations of you.

Each of us has our own mission in life to fulfill—our own path to follow. Regardless of our parents' best wishes, we must—if we are to be happy and fulfilled—follow that path.

In my workshops, I often ask the participants to write a paragraph about what their parents wanted for them. I have them title it: "What I Was Supposed to Be." For many, this exercise is an incredibly moving and inspiring experience. Consider what one executive wrote:

> I was supposed to grow up and be a wealthy lawyer or doctor who in his spare time led evangelistic crusades in the remote reaches of Africa. I was supposed to marry a lovely wife who would bear children, treat me like a prince, and revere my mother. I was supposed to live in the finest neighborhood where my parents lived (when I wasn't

preaching a revival in the African jungle), attend church regularly, and visit my parents weekly, but never ask them for money or to babysit my children.

Despite the fact that he had spent much of his twenties trying to fulfill these expectations, he has in his forties finally broken free to become the CEO of his own consulting company. He has a very close circle of friends, has never been married, and doesn't wish to have children.

Another moving paragraph came from a sixty year-old woman who attended another of my seminars. During a break, she came forward and said that writing the paragraph had been incredibly difficult for her. In fact, she said with tears in her eyes, she could only write one word: "invisible." That was all her parents had expected of her—to be a pleasant background in their lives. Whenever she tried to express herself and her needs, she was quickly reminded that children were to be "seen and not heard." She now told me with great sorrow in her voice, "I've spent much of my life trying to fulfill that expectation. Only now that I am in my sixties have I realized that I really do have some talent and a great deal to offer. I don't have to agree to be invisible." The agreement this woman kept most of her life is the agreement many people unconsciously keep.

> *What if you were to do this exercise? What would you say about your parents' expectations for you? How have these expectations shaped your life?*

Laurie Beth Jones, a successful motivational speaker and self-help author, writes of her parents' unfulfilled dreams:

> My father wanted to be a social worker, but after the War, he realized there would not be enough money to support a family, so he became a salesman instead. My mother was studying art at Pratt Institute in New York and had dreams of becoming an artist until the Depression hit. She became a bookkeeper instead, and for thirty-five years she worked with numbers instead of paintbrushes. Circumstances had come crashing down around my parents that seemed to shout NO! to their dreams. . . . I often wonder if their "unlived lives" became the tool that shaped me even more than the actual careers they chose."[1]

Your parents' unfulfilled dreams are a powerful force in your life. Even if you choose not to live those dreams for them, the guilt over not doing so can haunt you and steal your joy. Take some time now and write down all the dreams your parents had for their own lives. Now, write beside each one of their dreams how you may have tried to fulfill that dream for them. These may stem from agreements you have made with your parents that go something like this: "I love you and appreciate all the sacrifices you made for me when I was growing up. Since you had to give up your dream to take care of me, I will try to live your dream for you."

By making these agreements with your parents conscious, you can begin to choose whether or not these are dreams *for you*. Meditate on each one and ask yourself, is this dream really mine or is it my parents'? If you discover that many of these dreams are more your parents' dreams than your own, then find a specific way you can express your love for your parents that will support *them* in following *their dream*. It's never too late for someone to follow his or her passion. Maybe your parents have waited all their lives for someone to encourage and support them in following their dream. Instead of living it for them, you can give them the opportunity to live it for themselves and, in the process, free yourself to follow your own passion while giving something very precious to the parents you love.

2. Home Is Where My Parents Live

Do you think of "home" as where you currently live or where you lived with your parents when you were growing up? If the latter is true, you aren't alone and you are probably experiencing the crisis of individuation.

One of the biggest steps a child makes is leaving home and striking out on his or her own. Leaving home for the first time is a monumental occasion, one marked by both fear and excitement.

The truth is that even though you may have left home physically, it is quite another matter to leave home emotionally. In fact, some people never do. Their hearts remain tied to the place of their childhood and they never allow themselves to put down emotional roots elsewhere.

Bill and Margaret were born and raised in Dubuque, Iowa. After they graduated from the local high school, they both attended Clarke College in Dubuque, where Bill earned a degree in business. Bill struggled for several years to find a job in Dubuque, but the only offer he received was from a company in Des Moines, a day's drive away. Having no other options, Bill accepted the job and before he started, he and Margaret were married in the church where they both were raised.

Bill worked for the same company in Des Moines for over thirty years. During all that time, he and Margaret would return often to Dubuque, especially for holidays like Thanksgiving and Christmas, and spend them with Margaret's family. Margaret couldn't imagine not going "home" for the holidays. Even after she and Bill had a family of their own, they very rarely stayed in Des Moines for special occasions. When Bill finally retired, he and Margaret moved back to Dubuque.

Des Moines was never home for Margaret even though she spent much of her adult life there. She spent thirty years living in frustration and longing for the home she had left.

Sadly, Margaret's story isn't all that unusual. Many people—and perhaps you, too—think of home as a place where fond memories were made. Instead of allowing yourself to put down emotional roots in a new place, you cling to ties of where you once lived and the people you knew there.

Not a few marriages suffer greatly because one or both spouses refuse to psychologically move out of their parents' home. They cling to their childhood memories and emotional bonds, rather than moving on to a new place and new relationships. They spend a great deal of time keeping up with the old crowd, lingering over every piece of news that comes their way.

The real tragedy is that they never allow themselves and their marriages to grow past the limits of their childhood. By clinging to their childhood home, they stay stuck in the roles they assumed when they were children. Home is their parents' home, not their own. True friends are the friends they made in high school or college, but not those they have met in adulthood. Their lives differ very little from how they were when they left the place where they were born. What they do with their lives is a clear and obvious extension of what they were when they were younger. Consequently, they never allow themselves to experience the wonderful transformations that life has to offer anyone who is willing to learn and grow. More important, they never experience the peace and security that come from having a home of their own.

3. It Is Unloving of Me Not to Honor My Parents' Wishes

Some parents resist the attempts of their grown children to

establish a life of their own. Out of their own desire to be needed by their children, they continue to encourage, perhaps even insist, that their children defer to them on important life decisions.

When I was quite young, my parents did something very radical with our family: They decided to celebrate holidays at our home. Perhaps that doesn't sound so radical, but believe me, it sent shock waves through the Downs clan. My grandfather had always insisted that his children spend Christmas Eve, Fourth of July, and other significant days at his home. For many years, long after his children had children of their own, they all gathered at my grandfather's home. None of his children, including my parents, ever moved outside the small town where my grandfather and grandmother lived. (I can only imagine how controversial such a move would have been!)

So when my parents decided that we would spend holidays at our own home, it was nothing short of scandalous and took years for my grandparents to accept. Up until their deaths, I'm not sure that they ever really understood why we stopped spending all our holidays at their house.

Otherwise loving parents can sometimes act like my grandparents, using subtle (and sometimes not so subtle) manipulations such as guilt and pity to keep their grown children from establishing a life of their own. When this happens it can be incredibly difficult, even painful, for children to separate emotionally from their childhood need for their parents' approval.

Creating a life of your own isn't disrespectful to your parents or an unloving thing to do. It is something you *must* do if you are to be whole and happy. Their need to control you is about their own misplaced desires and isn't healthy for you. The truly healthy parent and grown child relationship is one in which the parent and the child become adult friends, each respecting the individuality of the other.

4. I Will Hide from My Parents Those Parts of My Life That My Parents Disapprove Of

This agreement is one that often takes place between a child and an adult who have different lifestyles. Perhaps the parent is a devout religious disciple and the child is not. Or the child is highly educated and the parent is not. Or the parent is straight and the child gay.

In any number of circumstances, it can seem easier to both the child and parent to agree not to discuss some area of the child's life. The child enters into this agreement to avoid the confrontation that he or she fears might lead to a loss of the parent's affection. The parent, not wanting a challenge from the adult child that might end disastrously, also enters into the agreement willingly.

While this may seem to be a rational, even productive way to maintain a relationship between parent and adult child, it isn't. The underlying assumption here is that the adult child isn't a free, responsible individual who should be respected as such. Instead, the adult child is forced to edit his or her life and hide certain aspects of his or her self. In some cases, such as that of the gay adult child, the child is forced to edit out an important portion of his or her life.

As an adult child you must ask yourself, "Why am I doing this?" What is the point of a relationship that isn't completely honest and open? What is it that your parents are loving if they're not loving the whole of you? It's really a false image of yourself that you've created to hold your parents' love and approval.

But what good is that approval if it isn't based on the real you? What good is partial love? If your parents can't accept the reality of you and you're willing to go along with it, then you must believe on some deep level that part of you isn't worthy of approval and love.

Your parents are no more perfect than you are. For them to insist that some aspect of your life must be hidden in order to maintain a relationship with them, they are acting in a cruel, abusive way. Perhaps it doesn't seem abusive, but the effect is no less damaging to your self-esteem and emotional well-being. That they brought you into this world doesn't give them the right to make you into their perfect image of a child.

Go ahead: Try a little brutal honesty with your parents. If you've held this agreement for a long time, at first you'll run into a lot of fear and anger, but if you'll stick with it, you'll likely discover that your parents will be somewhat relieved to know that they don't have to keep up the agreement any longer, either. It's far more stressful to keep pretending that something doesn't exist than to confront it and get past it.

More important, you'll gain a big leap in your own individuality. When you experience the joy of being yourself with the two people who have been the most powerful forces in your life, you gain a much stronger sense of identity and self-confidence. You can say to the rest of the world with ease and pride: *This is who I am*.

Love that is based on the reality of you is priceless. If you haven't experienced it with your parents, you never will until you give them the opportunity to know the real you. If you'll make that leap, you may be surprised how they rise to the occasion.

BECOMING AN INDIVIDUAL

The trance you have induced to avoid individuating is *dependency*. Instead of taking responsibility for yourself, you rely on your parents for direction in life. The trance of dependency not only happens with your parents, but it can grow to include significant others in your life. You may also become dependent upon a husband, wife, child, sister, minister, and so forth. When you learn how to induce the trance of dependency with your parents, you will easily transfer that trance to other strong or significant people in your life.

This is extremely important, so let me say it again: The trance of dependency is easily and often transferred to other important people in your life. You become dependent upon your spouse and feel you can't make decisions or even have an opinion without first consulting him or her. You "disappear" into the dependent relationship.

Why does the trance of dependency transfer so easily? Because inducing it becomes a life pattern that is learned and practiced from an early age. As you grow older, you easily slip into the dependent role with other authority figures, such as teachers or bosses, and meaningful people, such as spouses or children.

The trance of dependency is a pattern that you will repeat until you confront and resolve the crisis of individuation. Until you take responsibility for yourself and your decisions in life, you will always be looking for someone else who can tell you what to do. Long after your parents are gone, you will be dependent upon someone else.

The process of breaking the trance of dependency and moving toward resolution of the crisis of individuation is often slow, and it starts with small steps. One client of mine started by not having lunch every Sunday with her parents and instead agreed to have lunch when it was convenient for her and her family. Another client began calling her mother several times a week instead of every day.

While phone calls and regular lunches may seem harmless, they are the channels through which parents often control their children. They are regular sessions of subtle indoctrination of the parents' wishes. By decreasing those regular obligations, you are giving yourself more space to develop your own dreams and values.

For some, the controlling bond between parent and adult child is so strong that it is necessary for the child to distance himself or herself from the parents. When the parent is intent on not allowing the adult child to individuate, then distance may be the only answer, at least temporarily. By creating a controlled separation, the adult child has the opportunity to make decisions without the constant input of the parent. In doing so, the child begins to develop into an emotional adult.

This kind of separation can create short-term anxiety and even anger in both child and adult. Breaking such a strong bond is difficult and painful for a time.

The promise, however, is that if you individuate, the time will come when you can rebuild your relationship with your parents. Then you can approach them without the neediness, dependency, and resentment of a child, and instead love them for who they really are. They may still try to control your life, but you won't be susceptible to it. You'll see it for what it is— a misguided parent trying to do what he or she thinks is best for his or her adult child. You can honor their opinions and feelings without being obligated to agree with them.

Individuation is one of the most freeing experiences you will ever have. The road to resolution isn't easy and is at times filled with feelings of anxiety, abandonment, and fear, but the end result is the exhilaration of creating your own life.

You don't have to limit yourself to the life your parents want for you. You can create a life that fully expresses your individuality and reaches your highest potential, and in the end, that is the greatest honor you can give yourself . . . and your parents.

The Four Stages of the Crisis of Individuation

1. Breaking the trance of dependency

You create a trance of dependency—relying on someone else to tell you what to think and feel—to avoid having to grow up and be responsible for your own life.

2. Confronting the crisis

You acknowledge that you've allowed your parents (and others) to determine how you live your life.

3. Sorting through the confusion

You no longer defer to your parents' wishes. This can be very confusing and angering for parents who are accustomed to playing a dominant role in your life.

4. Resolving the crisis

You individuate, becoming independent and self-reliant.

I Want to Be in Control of My Life

[The Crisis of Fear]

At no point in your life were you as helpless and bewildered as the day you emerged from your mother's womb, and although you can't consciously remember that helpless experience or many of the others that followed it in those early years, they affect your life today.

No matter how loving and attentive your parents might (or might not) have been, you were completely dependent upon them for your survival during your earliest childhood. You were helpless to procure food, shelter, love, attention, touch, and everything else you needed in order to feel as safe and secure as you did in the womb.

The extent of the helplessness you felt and how your parents helped you meet your needs in great part determine how much you feel in control of your life today. If you were neglected and ignored, left to cry endlessly and suffer the consuming pains of hunger and loneliness, you carry that experience with you today, buried deep (and sometimes not so deep) within your unconscious. Whenever something happens to you that touches your buried helplessness, it elicits a reaction that is also rooted in your childhood experience. You call upon old patterns of behavior that worked for you as a child, such as *rage* (temper tantrum) or *denial* (daydreaming/sleeping).

Remembering and healing the helplessness of childhood is an important and difficult task. You don't *want* to remember that pain, and when you remember it, it can feel as if it will totally consume you, just as it did when you were an infant. The face of the inconsolable infant tells it all—the powerful need and the infant's awareness of his or her inability to fulfill it.

Lost in the public awareness campaign on child abuse and its devastating consequences is the equally important fact that even the best-cared-for infants and children experience painful feelings of helplessness and isolation outside the protective womb—it's just a factor of being alive. Even children who have parents who love and care for them cannot be shielded from the natural consequences of moving from the perfect, caring environment of the womb into the harsher reality of the world.

The childhood experience of helplessness starts at the moment of birth and continues until the child gains enough psychological strength to feel as if he or she can adequately meet all of his or her needs—a process that can extend well into adulthood for many people.

Particularly for those who were raised in abusive and emotionally unfulfilling environments, the experience of helplessness becomes one that is deeply internalized, and it is the starting point of a lifelong struggle to find some sense of control and emotional stability.

As an adult those situations that arouse your infantile help-lessness elicit a reaction that feels as if it is beyond your con-trol. You strike out, flee, rage, or depress yourself. You give yourself over to unconscious actions that are rooted in the helplessness that was experienced long ago, the helplessness that you never wish to experience again.

The situation that elicits this infantile helplessness is your "antagonist." Your antagonist controls you by forcing you to rebel against its collected evils. It pushes you from behind, pro-pelling you forward not of your own, chosen direction, but as an escape from pain. As long as your antagonist is controlling your life, you are definitely out of control. This is what the cri-sis of control is all about.

Your antagonist is the situation or scenario that makes you feel inadequate and fearful. While your antagonist was most likely born out your early life experiences, it is very real in the present moment. Regardless of where this sense of inadequacy and fear first emerged in your life, it is strongly influencing your life now. Your antagonist has become much more than the painful experience or experiences that created it; it is a powerful fear that controls you and keeps you stuck repeating the same painful patterns in life.

BETTY LYNNE'S ANTAGONIST

Betty Lynne spent much of her life rebelling against the pain she experienced at the hands of her father. Her father, a strict disciplinarian, had sexually abused her throughout much of her childhood. Remarkably, Betty Lynne was able to free herself from her father's control when she was a young teenager and eventually married a wonderful man and had several children of her own.

But Betty Lynne was haunted by what happened, not so much by the physical act of sexual abuse, as horrific as it was, but by the character traits of her father, the person who hurt her so deeply.

Whenever Betty Lynne found herself having to interact with a man who was controlling, moralistic, or overtly sexual, she would fly into a rage. As a result, throughout her life she had alienated many men who were integral to her and her family's well-being, such as her child's elementary-school principal, the family's minister, even the manager at her local grocery store. Something they did or said would unconsciously remind her of her father's strict rules and abuse of power, and all the rage she had stored inside would come spilling out. Most of the time it was over a little thing, such as her child not passing a test or the grocery store selling out of an advertised special. Her overreaction would often startle and anger those with whom she dealt. They took her reaction personally, unaware that what was really behind her anger had nothing to do with them. Betty Lynne herself was not sure where these feelings of extreme defensiveness and rage came from. She knew she was overreacting to the situation at hand, but she didn't seem to be able to stop herself.

For almost all her life, Betty Lynne had been hounded by her antagonist. She married her husband mostly because he was nothing like her father. She couldn't say that she was wildly in love with him, but he was kind and never tried to control her. Although religion had been very important to her early in life, she refused to attend any church because she thought most ministers were domineering men. She even refused to allow her son or daughter to play sports, and although she didn't admit it at the time, she later realized it was because men coached most sports. Even her career choice had been affected: She chose nursing because it was generally a "woman's" profession (she often had run-ins at work with the male doctors).

To say that Betty Lynne didn't like men wouldn't be true. There were times when she actually enjoyed the company of men—as long as they didn't in any way arouse the painful memories of the abuse she experienced from her father. In settings where she felt safe and in control, she enjoyed male companionship. Even at work, she found the male orderlies who worked for her to be very pleasant.

Only after Betty Lynne began to deal with her sexual abuse and the profound impact her father had upon her was she able to understand how those painful experiences had controlled her long after the abuse ended. Betty Lynne's antagonist had been in control for much of her life.

The feelings of helplessness that give birth to your antagonist can happen at any point in the early developmental stage of life. For many, those feelings of helplessness were acutely experienced in a school environment that was emotionally unsafe.

THE PLAYGROUND BULLY

Jason was a loner. He was shy but friendly although he never went out of his way to make new friends.

During his adolescent years, Jason had been a scrawny kid, the kind that all the other boys liked to pick on. Regularly he came home in tears, with torn clothing and black eyes. The nuns who ran the school where he attended never did much to intervene, even after his parents inquired about Jason's safety. They felt it might serve to "tough him up." His parents believed that the nuns, not Jason, should make decisions about his life. They valued the opinions of the nuns over the feelings of their child.

After many years of playground beatings, filled with taunting and teasing, Jason found some relief in high school. There he discovered that he had a talent for painting. His teachers were amazed at his ability. He even won a national art award that brought his school a great honor. Now he wasn't just the playground outcast and people were interested in what he could do!

But as Jason became an adult, his antagonist caused him to mistrust anyone who seemed powerful and self-assured. The world was a dangerous place in Jason's mind, and he was constantly on the lookout for those who might take advantage of him. He preferred to be by himself and make his art, the one thing that had always served him well.

Now in his mid-forties, Jason was lonely and feeling alienated. He wanted to have the kind of friends and relationships he saw everyone else enjoying, but he felt as if it was just something he wasn't capable of. Every time he started a relationship, he wondered how long it would be before he got hurt. True to his expectation, virtually all of his relationships ended in some sort of painful split, confirming his belief that the world was a dangerous place indeed.

When Jason was a child, his home life could hardly be called abusive by most standards, but it inflicted lifelong feelings of helplessness within him. His parents, devout Catholics, firmly believed that children should be taught the "right" way to be and that the opinions and feelings of their children had little bearing on what was "good for them." In many ways, this kind of childhood environment inflicted as much helplessness as an overtly abusive environment. The child was taught to ignore his own needs in favor of following the rules.

Many children are raised like Jason. In fact, children are the one class of people who are not considered capable of speaking on their own behalf. In all matters, the parents—not the child—are given the right to make decisions that affect the child's life.

Obviously, there is good reason not to allow an immature child to make decisions that might affect the rest of his or her life. But herein lies a problem: As a result, the child is not allowed to *control* his or her own life. It is out of this lack of control that the antagonist emerges.

Is there a specific incident or experience from your childhood that you can recall that still haunts you today? How has it affected your adult life?

BIG-BONED GIRL

Kama's mother had been a beauty queen when she was in college thirty years earlier. She was still thin and beautiful, looking half her real age. Kama, on the other hand, had inherited her father's big bone structure and propensity to be slightly overweight. During her formative years, Kama's mother encouraged her to eat less, exercise more, and "keep herself up." Maintaining her "ideal" weight and keeping her waist small was always a struggle for Kama and not one that she often won.

By the time Kama was in her mid-twenties she had been on more diets than she could remember. Her closet was jammed with three or four different wardrobes—ranging from smaller sizes (she bought those after going on a high-protein diet) to much larger ones. Now Kama was overweight and resigned to never being thin again.

Whenever Kama was around her mother, her feelings of guilt and shame escalated. She would rarely eat in front of her mother, and when she did, she ate sparingly. She never shopped for clothes with her mother and changed the subject when anything that was remotely related to weight came up between them.

WHAT'S YOUR ANTAGONIST?

Kama's antagonist attacks her with the fear of a poor body image. Betty Lynne's antagonist attacks her with the fear of men. Jason's antagonist attacks him with the fear of powerful others. Each of these antagonists brings up deep feelings of childhood helplessness that feel overwhelming and controlling. Their lives were controlled, not by their own intentions, but by unresolved powerful feelings that were rooted in the past.

Since all of us struggled with helplessness in our childhood, we all have an antagonist as an adult. What's is your antagonist? Is it your money? Your job? Your romantic relationships? Your parents? Your siblings?

Your antagonist is the one thing that has the power to make you feel truly helpless and can make you do things you wouldn't normally do. When you look back over your life, you can see the path of pain your antagonist has created for you. Your sense of inadequacy may have prevented you from taking

risks, making friends, finding a lover, starting a business, starting a family, or changing your life for the better. It kept you
paralyzed and unable to act in ways that you knew would
make your life better.

Remember Dale, the man whose frugality had almost
destroyed his marriage? His antagonist kept him acting in ways
that were counter to the things and people he treasured most
in life—and almost caused him to lose them for good.

Take a minute and list the times when you failed to do
something you knew would make your life better because you
were afraid. Try to come up with at least three instances.

♦ Did you fail to tell your spouse the truth about something
important for fear of rejection?

♦ Did you turn down a job opportunity because you were
afraid you might fail?

♦ Did you avoid making a connection with someone because
you were afraid he or she might not accept you?

♦ Did you destroy a relationship out of an unfounded fear of
betrayal or deception?

♦ Did you stop pursuing an important dream because you
feared you wouldn't be able to reach your goal?

Gaining control of your life requires that you face your
antagonist. If you are to resolve this crisis, you must discover
what is your antagonist.

As long as your antagonist is operating in the dark, unac-
knowledged corners of your mind, it pushes you to do things

you wouldn't normally do. You get angry, your weight yo-yos up and down, you suddenly quit your job, you have an affair, or you irreparably hurt your best friend.

IT'S ALL ABOUT FEAR

How is it that your internal antagonist can do this to you? Why does your internal antagonist control your life? Because you've induced the trance of *fear.*

The trance of fear swings into full force when you start telling yourself: "I'm doing all the wrong things, something bad is bound to happen." Again and again you tell yourself how worried you are, how scary the world really is, and what terrible things are just around the corner. The message of fear is quietly cunning, and the more you repeat it, the deeper the trance becomes. Before you know it, the trance starts invading your sleep and waking you in the night. The trance of fear is one of the most harmful trances you can induce.

When I think about how we induce the trance of fear, I think of how the infamous Rasputin betrayed the Russian monarchy shortly after the turn of the century. Rasputin was born a peasant in Siberia. By the age of thirty, he had left his family to become a wandering holy man. With little education and a seductive demeanor, Rasputin quickly gained a reputation for faith healing and debauched behavior. During a visit to St. Petersburg in 1905, Rasputin was presented at the court of Empress Alexandra, where he was able to relieve the suffering of her hemophiliac son, who was heir to the Russian throne. Enamored of Rasputin's supposed magical powers, Empress Alexandra made him a regular member of her entourage. When Emperor Nicholas II left St. Petersburg for the front lines of the Russian army during World War I, Rasputin wielded tremendous power over the empress and, consequently, over Russian politics. Under Rasputin's sway, she appointed many of his incompetent cronies to high government positions. In matters of both internal and foreign affairs, she sought and implemented his advice. Many historians believe that it was Rasputin's self-serving and flawed advice and his overwhelming influence over the empress that ultimately caused the czarist monarchy to fall.

You undermine yourself with the trance of fear just as the empress did with Rasputin. Fear lurks in the background constantly whispering misguided advice in order to keep the trance alive. It seems to be speaking for your own good, but in reality, it is betraying your confidence. It entices you to abandon your rational faculties and adopt other, fear-based decisions. If you allow it full rein, fear will eventually take control of your life.

Here's the crux of the matter: *You will never reach your highest potential until you learn to recognize that you have induced the trance of fear to avoid dealing with your antagonist.* Simply put, that's the breakthrough you're looking for. Once you learn to identify when you are in the trance of fear and know when it is telling you to do something, you can give yourself a choice to either give in to your antagonist or choose a way that is better for your well-being.

Rasputin met his fate when a group of Russian aristocrats discovered his untoward influence over the empress and assassinated him. So it is with your antagonist: You must uncover its subversive and fearful influence before you can eliminate its control over your life.

Your antagonist whispers in your ear:

- ◆ "Don't take a chance on him, he'll only hurt you."
- ◆ "Don't risk the money on starting a business, you'll only fail and lose it all."
- ◆ "Don't express yourself, people will just reject you even more."
- ◆ "Don't try to get ahead, you'll fail miserably."

Through the trance of fear, you convince yourself that your antagonist speaks truth. You should avoid these potentially disastrous situations. Over and over again you imagine the horrible consequences that might befall you and the terrible pain that could become yours. You transform the voice of fear into imagined good advice.

The trance of fear keeps you from confronting your antagonist. If you don't break this trance, it begins to color your life and decisions, affecting all of your behavior. It can provoke you to the extremes of passivity or aggression and can distort otherwise rational thinking. It rarely, if ever, inspires the best of decisions. Worst of all, it will take control of your life, while at the same time making you feel as if you have no control.

What does the trance of fear look, feel, and sound like in your life?

BREAKING THE TRANCE OF FEAR

The trance of fear is a tremendously difficult one to break. One of the ways to begin the process is to recognize some truths about fear that can be difficult to see while you are caught in its grip. Below are nine of the most important things to remember about the true nature of fear.

1. Fear Lives Only in the Mind

At first glance, this may seem painfully obvious, but take a minute to seriously consider the fact that fear does not exist in your environment—it lives solely in your head and heart. Fear is something that you do to yourself. No one can make you afraid except you.

Even though you know that fear is a mental and emotional thing, when you are acting upon fear, you often treat it as if it is something in your environment. It is as if your fear is created by what is happening to you (for example, "I am afraid because ———— is happening"). You convince yourself that fear is the only rational reaction to the situation, when in fact, it is mostly irrational.

2. Feeling Fear Is Not the Same Thing as Acting Upon Fear

There is a huge difference between *feeling* fear and *acting* upon fear. Risky situations elicit fear from everyone. We've all had certain scary experiences in life and certain events can call up within us the fear from those past experiences. It's nothing to be ashamed of, and is a completely natural response.

Acting upon fear is a different story. The feeling of fear tells you to do one thing: Get out of danger. Most often this means stopping and taking no action. In other words, fear teaches you to avoid the danger by not proceeding forward. Rather than take even the most intelligent risk, fear pushes you toward inactivity or escape. It asks of you, "Why take the risk?"

3. Even the Most Successful People Feel Fear

No matter how much experience or success a person has, from time to time he or she feels fear.

4. Fear Is About Imagined Catastrophes, Not Present Danger

Another distinct characteristic of fear is that it becomes an irrational belief in imaginary catastrophes rather than avoidance of true danger. In other words, fear is a continuing feeling of dread and panic. In your mind you enlarge the possibility of injury far beyond reality, to the point where you convince yourself that something very dire will happen if you do not take evasive action.

You tell yourself:

"Everyone must like me, *or* I will be alone and unloved."

"I must always be successful, *or* I will be a failure."

"I must constantly please the boss, *or* I will lose my job."

You create an exaggerated dichotomy in your mind: the desired outcome is ALL good, while every other outcome is EXTREMELY bad. You tell yourself that the desired outcome must be had, and you must avoid other outcomes at all costs. Notice how in the above fear statements the imagined consequences have become generalized and enlarged: "I will be alone and unloved." "I will be a failure." "I will lose my job." Fear is no longer about avoiding real dangers, but about avoiding *imaginary* catastrophes.

Fear feeds upon "what if" instead of "what is." At any point in life, the universe of what *could* happen is always larger than what is happening. There are an infinite number of possibilities, but only one present moment. Of all the things that could go wrong (or right), only one will happen. Fear begins to gain momentum when we give our attention to this surge of possibilities instead of to the present moment.

Conquering fear demands living in the present. Right now, what is happening? In this moment, what is the best I can do?

The epic movie *Titanic* gives a wonderful illustration of

how staying clearly focused on the present can conquer the madness of fear. In the final half-hour before the luxury liner turns vertical and slips into the water, the hero of the story, Jack, and his leading lady, Rose, struggle to escape the lower decks of the ship, which were filling quickly with water. As they encounter obstacle after obstacle in their struggle to stay above the water, Jack gives Rose clear, concise instructions that are focused on their present dilemma rather than upon the chilling possibilities of what might ultimately happen to them when the ship goes under. They focus on getting just one deck above the encroaching water. Once on the top deck, they focus on climbing to the end of the ship that is above the water. Then, they focus on clinging to the railing as it flips into the midnight air. Finally, they focus upon staying afloat after the ship has been completely submerged. Clearly, Jack and Rose's situation was dire. But attending to the horrible possibilities of what lay ahead would only have fueled their panic, immobilizing them, and further diminishing their chances for survival. Instead, they focused on each situation as it presented itself.

Other passengers, racked with fright, threw themselves off the upper decks to a certain death in the waters below. *Their fear forced them to create the very situation they were desperate to avoid.* Granted that the chances of survival for any of the remaining passengers was slim, it was even smaller for those who gave in to panic.

5. Fear Is a Breach of Trust in Yourself and Your Abilities

Not only does fear cause you to imagine dire traumas, *it keeps you continually doubting your ability to prevent or avoid these traumas.* In other words, when you engage in fear you lose faith in yourself and your abilities. It is a very destructive and irrational mind game we play with ourselves. Ironically, fear actually *causes* you to become the helpless creature you have imagined.

Fear is a breach of trust in your talents. Instead of knowing confidently that you have done your best (and it is enough), you doubt that your best is sufficient. You lose faith in your internal guidance system. Through fear, you chisel a crack in the wall of your self-confidence and peace of mind.

The truth is, you can't control all circumstances in any given situation. In fact, there is much in this world that is beyond your control. It is always possible that no matter how well you do a task, disaster could strike. Trusting yourself means that you know you have done everything you can possibly do to achieve the desired outcome. One powerful way to eliminate fear is to relinquish the outcome and trust in your talents. *You do your best and then let it go.* You set your eyes on a result and work to achieve it, but in the end you relinquish it, knowing that you have done all you can do *and it is enough.* By trusting your best effort, you inoculate yourself against fear.

6. Fear Grows in the Vacuum Created by Ignorance

Ignorance is another factor that feeds fear. The lack of knowledge about a situation is sufficient to cause you to fear, without any real danger being present. In the Middle Ages, mental patients were thought to be demon-possessed and were thrown out of their villages and forced to roam the wilderness searching for food. The deep sea was once thought to be inhabited by monsters that destroyed ships at will. American Indians were once feared as uneducable savages.

Today, we know all of this to be folklore, not reason for fear. As we have explored our world, other lands and other cultures, we have learned things we did not know before, and that knowledge has helped quell our fears.

Secrecy, whether intentional or not, creates ignorance, which, in turn, fuels fear. No better example of this exists than that of the assassination of President John Kennedy. The events surrounding the killing of Kennedy and the subsequent investigations by the Warren Commission were all shrouded in extreme secrecy, keeping the American public largely in the dark about the details of what occurred. That ignorance has fueled hundreds of fear-based books, conspiracy theories, and several major motion pictures blaming the Mafia, the FBI, the CIA, Cuban communists, and the U.S. government at large. The secrecy surrounding the assassination augmented our fears about the numerous potential masterminds behind the assassination.

Secrecy and ignorance are the antithesis of knowledge. Knowledge is indeed power: *The more we know, the less fuel there is for fear.*

7. Fear Is the Opposite of Growth

There is no such thing as a sure thing. Everything, no matter how regular or predictable, carries a risk. Modern physics has taught us that permanence is nothing more than a temporal illusion. Everything, at every moment, is in a state of flux. To believe that something is absolute and unchanging is to hold on to an illusion. To try to stop something from changing is to stop growing *and to start dying.*

The person who attempts to minimize all risks is doomed not to get the best out of life. This is the person who won't make a business proposal until he has watered it down with everyone's ideas. This is also the person who won't allow herself to pursue a romantic relationship for fear of being rejected. They are always staying on the safe path—one that, in reality, is the path of fear.

In a 1997 interview, Katharine Graham, publisher of the *Washington Post,* told of her early years at the helm of the newspaper. Thrust unexpectedly into the chief decision-making role at the *Post* after her husband's suicide, she remembers how she tried to quell her fears by gaining everyone's approval for her decisions. She made the rounds with each decision, trying to win the blessing of all the major players at the newspaper. But those decisions, she remembers, were not the best of her career. Later on, after she conquered her fear, she would seek her staff's input, but when the time came, she made her own decision.[1]

8. Acting on Fear Can Create a False Sense of Relief

One of the properties of fear that makes it so difficult to break is that it perpetuates itself. For example, when you are afraid and take action to alleviate fear, you feel a sense of relief. That sense of relief gives you the feeling that you have done the right thing, when all you have really done is alleviate your feeling of fear. So what are you likely to do the next time you are afraid? Immediately act to alleviate the fear so you can feel the relief.

The important point is that what brings you relief isn't solving the situation *but is only alleviating the fear.* In other words, your decision is driven by what will reduce the feeling of fear rather than what is the best decision given the situation. In this way, fear becomes a self-sustaining system that can keep you stuck within its confines.

9. Fear Often Attracts What It Attempts to Avoid

Earlier in this chapter I mentioned that when we act upon fear we tend to create the situation we actually fear. In other words, fear tends to attract what is feared.

One of the lessons every aspiring equestrian learns is that when you are thrown from a horse, the best thing you can do is to immediately get back on. Why? Because a rider who doesn't get back on the horse becomes a fearful rider. And that can be dangerous. You see, horses (like people) have an incredible ability to sense fear, so when they sense the person riding them is afraid, they often react with rough behavior. That, of course, only reinforces the rider's fear, causing the horse to continue misbehaving. And the cycle continues. By pushing through the fear by getting back into the saddle, the rider is able to calm his or her fears and, in turn, is able to calm the horse he or she is riding.

Fear will make you act in ways that actually create what you are trying to avoid. Examples of this abound:

◆ Muggers often attack those whom they perceive to be most afraid of them.

◆ A fearful performer is usually too nervous to give a good performance, and consequently fails miserably.

◆ A suspicious and fearful person creates such an uncomfortable environment in a relationship that the other person eventually leaves.

◆ A fearful parent acts in overbearing ways that push a child into a rebellious frame of mind, causing the child to act out in harmful ways.

What has fear prevented you from doing in your life?

OVERCOME BY FEAR

Not all that long ago, I served on the board of a nonprofit organization whose executive director destroyed her promising career in this very manner. Shortly after I joined the board of directors, the nonprofit agency hired a new executive director. The candidate who was hired was perfectly qualified on paper to do the job and had stood above all the other candidates from the national search. Her name was Susan and she had a great deal of experience and a good education and was very engaging. Everyone involved in the organization felt that Susan was perfect for the job.

Unfortunately, before taking her new job, Susan spoke extensively with a former, disgruntled staff member. This person warned her about all of the people who might "undermine" her, and all the possible ways that she could fail. Susan apparently internalized much of this information and started her new job with a deep suspicion that some of the staff would be working against her. Outwardly she seemed to be as accommodating and supportive as could be expected, but she kept a wary eye on those she thought might not support her.

Within months of her hiring, staff members began to quit. At first the exodus wasn't really alarming, since this often happens when a new manager is installed in an organization. Each person who left had a reason. One had a new job, another wanted to work from home—all the usual reasons why people leave. Six months after Susan's hiring, however, the exodus was still continuing, and it was more than just staff members.

Other agencies that worked closely with the organization began to refuse to participate in our programs, and local community leaders who were critical to our mission began to be less enthusiastic about our organization.

Nine months into Susan's tenure, those of us on the board really became concerned. Here was a person who seemed to be doing all the right things and yet everything was slowly falling apart. Worst of all, donations were tapering off, and we were headed into troubled financial waters. I began meeting regularly with Susan to discover what was happening, and over time a picture of fear began to emerge. Susan had come to this job fearing the worst, and slowly but surely she was creating what she feared.

When she and I talked about former staff members who had quit, she mentioned that she hadn't done much to encourage them, because after all, "They didn't support her vision for the organization." When we discussed the lack of involvement with other agencies, she said that she suspected a few of them had been trying to hire away our best staff members (and, in fact, they had hired one of our best fundraisers) and consequently had broken off those relationships. As for the decreased involvement with community leaders, she had some equally fearful excuse about why she had discouraged those relationships.

After her first year, the board initiated a standard review of Susan's performance by asking all the board members to rate her job performance. The results, which weren't stellar but were not all that bad, were then given to Susan. Surprisingly, she resigned after receiving the feedback.

Needless to say, we were all shocked at her sudden departure. What we uncovered in the weeks that followed was that Susan had interpreted every bump in the road as an attempt to "undermine" her leadership. It seems that each bump became more evidence in her mind of others trying to undermine her.

I contacted former staff members and discovered that several had quit because Susan had constantly interfered with their jobs—second-guessing their decisions and overriding their conversations with clients. When they had complained about this to her, she only seemed to start interfering more. Finally, they had had enough and quietly left the organization. Apparently, Susan had twisted their feedback to her into evidence that they truly weren't supporting her, so she had become even more vigilant in supervising their work. When they quit the organization, she was relieved instead of being greatly concerned with the critical loss of talented manpower. The final straw for Susan had been the board's evaluation of her performance, which only confirmed her growing fears. Not only was the staff against her, so was the board! All the board members agreed that it wasn't that at all—but through the lens of fear, it appeared that way to Susan. The bottom line was this: Susan's fear of rejection actually created the situation she thought she was avoiding.

Breaking the cycle of fear requires that you deliberately stop *acting out* your fear. Even though you continue to feel it, you push through it. You get back up on the horse that threw you, put on your brave face, and keep pushing forward.

Earlier in this chapter you made a list of the ways you act

out of fear. Now, take that list and create companions to those fears. Write down positive actions you can take despite your fears. They don't have to be monumental acts, just ones that are simple and doable. For example, if one of the fears you wrote down is that you are afraid that acquaintances you have will reject any advances you make toward becoming friends, one possible step might be to ask one of those people out to lunch. The important thing is that no matter how small the step, you take *action* to fight against your fear.

> *What positive actions can you take to begin breaking the cycle of fear?*

The truth is that once your antagonist is met squarely and you don't turn to run, you will resolve your crisis: When you face your antagonist and don't try to escape, the antagonist will begin to fade away. It's simple and amazingly profound. Your antagonist does not have innate power—it is your attempts to escape and avoid your antagonist that give it power to hurt you. When you stand your ground, even when it takes every bit of strength you can summon, your antagonist is forced to retreat. If you stand unflinching long enough, the antagonist will disappear for good.

The Four Stages of the Crisis of Fear

1. Breaking the trance of fear

You create a trance of fear—situations that remind you of your antagonist—to avoid dealing with painful memories.

2. Confronting the crisis

You acknowledge that you've allowed your antagonist to shape your life.

3. Sorting through the confusion

You begin to stop avoiding situations even though they make you fearful.

4. Resolving the crisis

As you push through the fear, you begin to feel it less and less as it loses its power over you.

What Does It All Mean?

[THE CRISIS OF SPIRITUAL MEANING]

Personal tragedy is almost always the precursor of your spiritual crisis. That's what happened for a whole city one dark morning in Oklahoma.

On April 19, 1995, I stood mesmerized in front of an old black-and-white television in a bicycle shop near the French Quarter of New Orleans. I normally rode my bike the three-mile trip from my home to my office when the weather was nice, as it was that day, but this time, I had a flat tire and had to walk my bike over a mile to the nearest repair shop. What was so different about that day wasn't the flat tire, but the shocking pictures that were flashing across the television screen. A large building in Oklahoma City, it seemed, had been bombed, and the rescuers were carrying the bodies out of the rubble. Worst of all, it seemed that many of the casualties were small children.

It wasn't until I reached my office and took a phone call from my older sister that I learned that the building I had seen on television was the Federal Building in Oklahoma City where my younger sister, Amy, worked. No one seemed to know whether she was injured, dead, or alive. No one had seen her, including her husband, who had rushed to the scene. We were all in shock.

Sometime around three o'clock that afternoon we received the call: Amy had been rescued from the building's basement (she was on the fourth floor when the bomb went off) and was now in the back of an ambulance speeding toward a local trauma center. Luckily, she was alive, conscious, and not too badly hurt.

In the days that followed, the extent of the senseless tragedy began to hit us all, especially the unfortunate survivors who lost family, friends, and worst of all, children. Over twenty children from the daycare center were killed. At the Federal Employee's Credit Union where Amy worked, eighteen of the thirty-two employees were lost. Spouses, children, parents, and grandparents were all left with the haunting question: "Why?"

In the years that followed that tragedy the survivors of the bombing were faced with some of the darkest days of their lives. They wrestled with questions such as:

◆ "Why was I spared while others were not?"

◆ "Why were so many innocent babies killed?"

◆ "What kind of God would allow this to happen to a peaceful, religious community?"

◆ "Why did God choose some for death and not others? Does this mean that there is no God and that this was a totally random act of violence?"

At some point in your life you will wrestle with these same difficult questions, just as the survivors of the bombing did. As in the Old Testament story of Jacob wrestling with the angel for a blessing, you will struggle with life's difficult circumstances and demand to know what it is all about. What *does* it all mean?

There will come a time in your life when you need to *experience* the spiritual. Not have a theology, or reunite with your family's religious traditions, but really *feel* a connection with something bigger than yourself. When this happens, you are ready for a spiritual awakening.

The more invested you are in the realms of intellect or practical thinking, the harder this crisis will be for you to confront. "Who, me? I don't believe in any of that stuff. 'Right now' is the only thing that counts. I don't believe in or need the spiritual." In some circles it's even fashionable to be dismissive and skeptical about spiritual matters, and it is considered a sign of mental weakness if one publicly explores his or her spiritual crisis.

But the truth is, every one of us believes that we are somehow connected to all other human beings, and indeed, to all of creation. We all believe in a power greater than ourselves (even if that power can be explained scientifically), and we hunger to experience that power in a greater way than we do now. The need to understand and experience the spiritual is with us from birth.

Wilder Penfield was a skeptic most of his life. He was educated at Princeton, Oxford, and Johns Hopkins, and his training as a neuroscientist had convinced him that everything about human consciousness could be traced back to the brain. His experiments led to some of the most groundbreaking research on the brain. During brain surgery when the skull was partially removed, he would apply electrical stimulation to each part of the brain and ask his patient to describe the effect (the patients were awake but felt little discomfort because the brain doesn't directly experience pain). Penfield was one of the first scientists to map the functions of the brain in this way. Excited by his findings, he predicted that one day all aspects of human behavior would be directly related to some specific part of the brain. The significance of this was profound for the time—if the brain could account for all behavior, did that mean there was no soul? At the time, Penfield believed science would soon eclipse all notions of spirituality and religion.

But, hard-minded scientist that he was, Penfield couldn't escape his own spiritual crisis. After fifty years of research and a deep personal crisis, he changed his mind. As he said in his last work, *The Mystery of the Mind,* "I came to take seriously, even to believe, that the consciousness of man, the mind, is NOT something to be reduced to brain mechanism." Later in the book he writes, "For myself, after a professional lifetime spent in trying to discover how the brain accounts for the mind, it comes as a surprise now to discover, during this final examination of the evidence, that the dualist hypothesis (the idea that the mind is separate from the brain) seems the more reasonable of explanations.... What a thrill it is, then, to discover that the scientist, too, can legitimately believe in the existence of spirit!"[1]

What Does It All Mean?

Even if you're a skeptic like Walter Penfield, you will discover that your spiritual crisis will not be satisfied by trying to intellectually reason it away. No matter how many "reasons" you discover, no matter how smart or well-educated you might be, you will always hunger for some kind of spiritual awakening. You will not be satisfied until you are willing to open yourself up to your own spiritual nature.

Can you remember a time when you had a spiritual experience? What was the situation? How did it happen? What did it feel like?

A REASON FOR BEING

What reason do you have to hope? What reason makes it all worthwhile?

If this plane of existence is all there is, and the only true reason for living is to experience as much pleasure as possible, life is bleak indeed. And suffering—an unavoidable part of living—becomes totally senseless and futile.

The spiritual crisis comes at the time in life when you begin to question your connection to something bigger in the universe, and as you wrestle with this, you may be flooded with a sense of hopelessness and futility. You question your most essential beliefs about life, love, and your role in the big scheme of things. It is a thorny and dark time when you must answer the most difficult question of all: What reason do I have to live?

Because this crisis is so dark and threatening, you may spend much of your life avoiding it, shoving the burning questions to the back of your mind, and trying your best not to grapple with their tricky implications. You are terrified that the answer you may find is that there is no real reason to live. Rather than live with that answer, you tell yourself it is better not to ask the question.

The spiritual crisis is the most tenacious of all the crises you will experience. It will likely come to you in the midnight of a tragic season of your life. It is at those times, as it was for those after the Oklahoma City bombing, that you wrestle with the ultimate meaning of your life.

What makes this crisis so difficult, more so than all the others, is that only *you* can discover the resolution to this crisis. No one can give you the answer. No one can solve this riddle for you. Only you can answer it for yourself, and the only answer that will work for you must be *experienced*.

Are you disappointed? Do you wish for a guru, a teacher, a spiritual leader who can give you the ultimate truth containing the definitive reason for your life? If you do, you're certainly not alone. That's exactly where everyone who is struggling with this crisis begins—looking for the one answer that will make it all worthwhile.

If there truly is a spiritual crisis and it is something every-body experiences, why are there so many skeptics in the world declaring spirituality to be hogwash? If this crisis does truly exist, why do so many of us avidly avoid dealing with it?

One of the common trances you may have induced to avoid dealing with your spiritual crisis is *religiosity.* You induce this trance when you accept nicely packaged answers to very deep and important questions about the nature of your life and its place in this universe. Instead of fighting for your own soul, you try to hide behind the vestiges of someone else's struggle.

Are you surprised, maybe even a little offended by what you're reading? While it's true that religion can be very helpful to you in resolving your spiritual crisis, the trance of religiosity is using religion to give you all the answers without any question or doubt. No one human being or philosophy can give you all of the answers to your life—they can only guide you toward discovering those answers for yourself. You've got to do the work of confronting your own crisis and finding the resolution.

Religion is certainly meant to be a guide and a comfort to you during your spiritual crisis. The problem is that too many of us use religion to *escape* from spiritual crisis rather than to deal with it. It's easier to accept the answers handed to us by someone who is officially religious than it is to really acknowledge the crisis of meaninglessness that burns within our own souls.

Unfortunately, even some men and women of the cloth have the misguided notion that all there is to spirituality is the religious trance. They focus on all the hypnotic elements of religion—the dark sanctuaries, the mesmerizing stained glass, the angelic hymns, the bone-rattling organ music, the repetitive bowing, kneeling, and chanting, and the rhythmic sing-song delivery of a sermon or lesson. These religious hypnotists attract large congregations of people hoping to avoid dealing with their spiritual crisis, and they come every week to have their dose of the religiosity trance.

Inducing a type of trance from time to time can be very helpful in your spiritual search. It reminds you of your spiritual side and the need you have for spiritual fulfillment. Using this kind of trance through daily meditation or prayer may become an essential part of your spiritual practice.

The trance of religiosity is a very different thing. It is a trance that you live without questioning—a prescribed belief system and a way of life that you accept without thinking about it. This kind of trance is an escape from crisis, not a path to enlightenment. The trance of religiosity can occur with virtually any spiritual path, new or ancient. There are plenty of people who leave traditional religions, seeking answers to their spiritual crisis, only to find themselves inducing the same trance of religiosity with some new form of religion. Whether it's ancient scriptures or a living guru giving you the answers, if you accept those answers unquestioningly, you are inducing the trance of religiosity.

*How have you used the religiosity trance to avoid
dealing with your own spiritual crisis?*

There are several unnatural agreements that may be keeping you from resolving your spiritual crisis.

1. I Will Follow My Parents' Religion

Unfortunately, while those simple, untried answers handed
you by the religion of your parents may work, they aren't your
answers, and until you've wrestled with them intimately, they
never will be. In other words, you can't know the reason for
your life until you allow yourself to go through the full fury of
your spiritual crisis. It is a storm that will rock your life to the
core, probably causing you to doubt virtually everything
you've ever believed to be true. For a while, this crisis will
leave you bewildered, frightened, and terribly confused, and
there's no way around it. Traditional religious paths can nurture
your soul, but only after you have personally struggled with
the truths they offer.

Viktor Frankl was certainly one of the most compassionate scholars of human behavior to grace modern psychology.
Frankl was an accomplished Jewish psychiatrist who lived in
Austria before World War II. During Hitler's horrendous mur-
der of millions of innocent Jews, Dr. Frankl was sent to several
concentration camps and eventually landed in the dreaded

Auschwitz. His wife and family were all killed, while he endured unbearable hunger, disease, and excruciating torment at the hands of his captors.

What is so remarkable about Viktor Frankl's life wasn't his suffering, but how he handled that suffering, still finding the time and energy to comfort those around him who had lost all hope. Never did he take the easy path of "lying down to die." Instead, he held fast to his strong belief in God and the purpose of his life in helping others.

After the war Dr. Frankl was set free and began to teach the world about the absolute importance of the spiritual crisis. He wrote in his last book before his death:

> They [religious believers] often depict, not to say denigrate, God as a being who is primarily concerned with being believed in by the greatest possible number of believers, and along the lines of a specific creed, at that. "Just believe," we are told, "and everything will be okay." But alas, not only is this order based on a distortion of any sound concept of deity, but even more importantly it is doomed to failure: Obviously, there are certain activities that simply cannot be commanded, demanded, or ordered, and as it happens, the triad "faith, hope, and love" belongs to this class of activities that elude an approach with, so to speak, "command characteristics." Faith, hope, and love cannot be established by command simply because they cannot be established by will. I cannot "will" to believe, I cannot "will" to hope, I cannot "will" to love—and least of all can I

"will" to will. . . . Nowhere, to my knowledge, is this brought home to us more strikingly than with the uniquely human phenomenon of laughter: You cannot order anyone to laugh—if you want him to laugh, you must tell him a joke.[2]

What Dr. Frankl discovered is that your spiritual crisis cannot be resolved simply by dissolving yourself in your parents' beliefs or by adopting some other packaged set of religious convictions. You cannot will yourself to believe in any particular meta-idea. In order to have a true spiritual experience, it must be organic—*it must spring directly from your heart and daily experience.*

If you try to avoid this crisis by "willing" yourself to believe "unquestioningly" in a set of spiritual principles, you will actually find yourself deeper in spiritual crisis. For example, those who had not resolved their spiritual crisis before experiencing the Oklahoma City bombing had the most difficult time afterward coming to terms with what had happened. Five years after that traumatic experience, many of them still struggled with understanding it and had lost all faith and hope in what they formerly believed. The truth was, their former beliefs weren't really theirs, and the tragedy of the bombing wrenched those borrowed beliefs from their hands.

Dr. Frankl found this to be true in Auschwitz, too: "One might say that just as the small fire is extinguished by the storm while a large fire is enhanced by it—likewise a weak faith is weakened by predicaments and catastrophes, whereas a strong faith is strengthened by them."[3]

> *Write down your most important spiritual beliefs.*
> *How many of these beliefs have you found to be true*
> *through personal experience? How many have been*
> *"handed down" by your parents/religious tradition?*

2. God Must Be a Lot Like My Parents

Another spiritual dead end on the road to resolving your crisis is to base your beliefs on your parents' personality. In other words, to create your image of God (the Universe, Allah, and so forth) based upon your image of your parents. For example, if your parents were loving, supportive, and nonjudgmental, you might automatically accept spiritual beliefs that reflect a deity with those qualities. Likewise, if you experienced parents who were withholding, emotionally distant, or maybe even abusive, your experience of spirituality might reflect this. Such a painful childhood might very well lead you to bury your spiritual needs deep within and proclaim yourself to be a true agnostic (that is, one who believes in nothing that is spiritual).

The Swiss psychoanalyst Alice Miller has spent much of her life working with people who were abused in childhood. One of her clients, Inge, quite eloquently described her crisis like this:

It says in the Bible we should not make any graven images. Why not, actually? Why is God allowed to see all our weaknesses, to read our most secret thoughts without our being able to stop Him, and to punish and persecute us for having them, while only *His* weaknesses must remain invisible? Has He no weaknesses? If God is Love, as I was taught, then He certainly should feel free to show Himself. We would learn from His love. Does He hide Himself, or is He hidden by those who made an image of Him using their fathers as a model, and passed it on to us? . . . Perhaps the theologians are not in a position to create an ideal image of true goodness and omnipotence differing from the character of their real fathers until they have seen through this character. And so they create an image of God based on the model they are already familiar with. . . . Perhaps they could imagine other, similarly anthropomorphic images of God if they had had a different childhood.[4]

Regardless of whether you create a loving or a vengeful image of God, if you are using your parents as the model, that image will fall completely apart during the heat of your spiritual crisis.

What is your image of God? How has this image developed over time?

3. Spirituality Is Something You Only Need to Worry About Before You're About to Die

Real spirituality connects you to all of creation, and it isn't solely about earning brownie points for heaven. In other words, a belief system that is only based on earning eternal life, with no guide or insight regarding life here on earth, will *never* survive a spiritual crisis. That's a belief system that is controlling you, not one that is feeding your soul.

Pie-in-the-sky, fear-based religion was created to control you, not to help you live a more loving and fulfilled life. Gore Vidal, the eminent American essayist, expresses this truth eloquently in his essay "The Tyranny of the Sky God." Vidal traces the roots of religion that is based *solely* on earning rewards in heaven to power-hungry men who desperately wanted to control the masses. By creating and sustaining a religious system that denied earthly comforts for rewards in heaven, these men could control the otherwise unruly masses, forcing them into hard work and personal sacrifice. By promising heaven for good behavior, they could convince their underlings to produce and not rebel or complain.

The kind of religion Vidal describes is one that is based on fear. Fear of eternal punishment. Fear that you aren't good enough. Fear of an angry God. That kind of religion leads you to become hard and judgmental of yourself and those around you.

True spirituality focuses on what you can do *today* to improve your life and the lives of others. While it may include ideas about the next life, that isn't the only focus. Rather it is just a part of the big picture.

Charlene grew up with a father who was a strict disciplinarian. He laid down the rules and expected his children to unquestioningly follow them. His standard response was "You do this because I told you to do it!" She was required to attend church twice a week and to live by the tenets of her father's hellfire-and-brimstone beliefs.

When Charlene became a young woman, she married a man who held her father's beliefs, and they set about raising a family the same way. Everything they did was about avoiding hell and earning the favor of God, who would admit them into heaven when they died.

That system worked for them until a drunk driver killed their five-year-old son. Charlene was devastated and grew bitter in the years following her son's death. Everyone else seemed to be living a life of sin, but their children survived. Why was her child taken from her? The drunk driver was clearly a sinner and he survived. Why did God spare his life?

In the years following that tragic accident, Charlene's marriage also fell apart. Slowly, she had pushed her husband out of her shattered life, until the day came when he couldn't take her bitterness and anger any longer and left. Now, her child was gone and so was her marriage.

It was the divorce that finally pushed Charlene to go for counseling. She desperately wanted to be the person she was before the accident, but couldn't seem to feel anything. She was angry with her husband, the drunk driver, and most of all with God for letting this happen to her. He (God) had destroyed her whole life—despite the fact that she had done all the right things.

Charlene's counselor, a wise and spiritual woman herself, gently helped Charlene to examine her beliefs. Maybe religion wasn't just about saving up "brownie points" so that bad things wouldn't happen to her. Maybe spirituality was more about finding joy and peace in this life than about simply waiting and hoping for the life to come.

It took years of help for Charlene to loosen the grip of the fear-based religion she had learned at her father's knee. In time, she found a new spiritual path for herself, one that saw God as a helper to *all* people, not just those who attended her church and professed the same beliefs. Her new spirituality transformed her anger into a greater understanding of the meaning of suffering and the importance of loving in the present moment. She had wasted many years being angry over her son's death; she had completely ignored the other important people in her life. Now, loving others and enjoying what God had given her today became her focus. If only she had known this when her son was alive! But now she had learned the lesson, and she wasn't about to let another beloved person in her life depart without her having cherished that person as much as she was able to.

As in Charlene's case, a fear-based, it-will-all-be-better-in-heaven philosophy won't survive your spiritual crisis. The day will come when you need a spirituality that can help you make the world a better place right now. This is a spirituality that helps you heal your suffering and doesn't teach that your suffering will be your ticket into heaven. Love for others and for the planet will always be one of the cornerstones of your true spiritual path.

THRUST INTO CHAOS

The onset of your spiritual crisis can happen in many ways, but the two most common triggers are the loss of someone you love or a particularly traumatic physical experience, such as a prolonged and difficult childbirth or a near-death accident.

In times like these, when great suffering is involved, we begin to search for the bigger reason for our lives. Making sense of our own suffering pushes us to begin our spiritual journey. How does *this* fit into the bigger picture? What is the bigger picture?

After the Oklahoma City bombing, those who experienced it directly and even those who were simply near it were deeply shaken by the tragedy. Ministers', rabbis', and therapists' offices were packed with people desperately seeking answers to questions they had never asked before. Hundreds of counselors were brought in from all areas of the country to help handle the demand for answers. People were demanding to know: Why did this happen? Could it happen to me? What does it mean?

THE JOURNEY BEGINS

The secret to resolving your spiritual crisis is to open yourself up to experiencing a connection to something that is larger than yourself and that transcends your own ego needs. There are many paths to experiencing this connection, but the *experience* is crucial to your happiness.

Jung called it the "collective unconscious"; Frankl called it the "superconscious"; spiritualists call it the "spirit world"; Jesus called it "the kingdom of God within you"; and Hollywood has most recently called it "the sixth sense." Whatever name is applied and whatever path it evokes, the common elements of the fruitful spiritual journey come from access to that part of you that is also a part of everyone else on this planet. It is the spiritual connection we all share.

Once you've begun your spiritual journey, the key to maintaining and growing in your experience of the spiritual connection lies in practice. Like a muscle, you must exercise your spiritual sense often to keep it tuned and working properly. You've got to use your spirituality.

Once when I was in graduate school, all the students in my program were required to attend a seminar with a famous researcher of hypnosis. Thinking that hypnosis was nothing more than nonsense held over from the nineteenth century sideshows of Anton Mesmer (one of the first hypnotists and the root of the word "mesmerized"), we reluctantly attended. Of course, we were all *just too* sophisticated to be hypnotized!

How wrong we were! It wasn't long after Dr. Barber began his lecture that he stopped, looked at the audience of faculty and graduate students in psychology, and proclaimed that he had successfully hypnotized half the room. Shocked, we looked around, and sure enough, half the room was staring forward with trancelike glazes over their faces. He then proceeded to demonstrate the importance and value of altered states of consciousness like hypnosis for mental health professionals, using the hypnotized audience members.

Hypnosis, like regular prayer and meditation, induces an altered state of consciousness. These altered states are essential to practicing your spirituality, and virtually every spiritual path employs some form of altered state. An altered state of consciousness allows you to filter out much of the static of your day-to-day life and enables you to experience your connection to all of creation. And the more you do it, the more comfortable you become in that realm and the more at peace you grow with the meaning of your life. You must suspend the chatterbox of your mind and enter into a completely different state of mind in order to nurture your spiritual nature.

Whether you spend quiet time in a garden, walk through the woods, meditate in your room, pray, or practice self-hypnosis, your spiritual nature hungers for these times of nurturing. Regardless of the practice you choose, this is a time for you to set aside the demands of your current reality and to feed your soul.

One thing that is absolutely clear about the successful resolution of your spiritual crisis is that it should lead you to become a more loving person. Love is the ultimate spiritual practice. Regardless of whom you study, and what if any religious tradition you explore, you will find that those who successfully resolve their spiritual crisis become more loving and compassionate on their earthly journey.

True spirituality will also not separate you from others. It will cause you to reach out and embrace the world around you. If your path leads you to think of yourself as fundamentally separate, different, more enlightened, or better than the rest of humankind, you've gone off track. The resolution of your spiritual crisis should be rooted in the experiential knowledge of love. When you have experienced unconditional love, it has the power to transform your life completely. The seeming futility of life melts away, and you find the one and only reason to live.

> *How do you practice your spirituality? Are there practices you've intended to keep, but haven't? What can you do to make spirituality more a part of your everyday life?*

To start you on the path to resolving your spiritual crisis, agree to do at least one of the following during the next week:

◆ Spend some time in complete quiet and meditate. Start with ten minutes a day and find the amount of time that feels right for you.

◆ Visit a church or place of worship that means something to you.

◆ Start reading a book on a spiritual tradition or practice.

◆ Spend an hour or two with someone who has a spiritual practice and talk with that person in depth about his or her beliefs and practices.

The Four Stages of the Crisis of Spiritual Meaning

1. Breaking the trance of religiosity

You create a trance of religiosity—relying on someone else to give you the answers to the question of life's meaning—to avoid having to struggle with the answers yourself.

2. Confronting the crisis

You acknowledge that there is a bigger meaning to life than you've allowed yourself to experience, and that you cannot simply take someone else's answers as your own.

3. Sorting through the confusion

You begin to explore your spiritual side, perhaps by studying different spiritual traditions and practices.

4. Resolving the crisis

You begin to feel a greater connection to the world around you and you start to find a sense of purpose in life.

This Isn't What I Dreamed It Would Be

[THE CRISIS OF BROKEN DREAMS]

Your life will never be the life you once imagined it would be. It will not be the life you dreamed of as a child, nor the life you heard about in fairy tales and television stories. It will not be the life you imagined when you graduated from school or married. Things just won't turn out that way.

Somewhere down the line, a divorce happens, a parent dies, you are promoted out of your dream job, you can't afford your dream house, your children aren't good students, and you have to work harder than you ever imagined to keep your life going. How did this happen?

The day this fact hits you in the gut is a crisis day. You wonder what has gone wrong, where you got off track, and you are overcome with a feeling that you must make drastic changes, *and now!*

Let me tell you a well-kept secret: No one's life turns out like he or she planned it. *No one's.* Former President Bill

Clinton may have always planned on being president, but he surely didn't plan on the possibility of being impeached or on being the butt of locker-room jokes. Greg Louganis planned to become an Olympic gold medal diver, but he never imagined becoming a spokesperson for HIV-infected people. Christopher Reeve dreamed of being on stage, but not in a wheelchair as an advocate for those with spinal cord injuries. And you . . . your life will not be the dream you imagined either.

So are dreams possibly harmful to you? Is it wrong to want the best life possible? Of course not. Dreams are what inspire you to reach for the best and sometimes achieve it. Without dreams, your life would lack inspiration.

The crisis of broken dreams centers on three very important realizations: First, not all of your dreams will come true; second, some of the dreams that do come true will not feel as good as you imagined they might; third and most important, *your happiness isn't dependent on your dreams' coming true.*

Many of us grew up thinking that real happiness could only be ours if our ultimate dream came true in life. If it didn't, we'd either spend our life trying to make it come true or we'd become a total loser, bitter and defeated. In all those fairy tales spun out of Hollywood that you and I grew up watching, the message was clear: My happiness depends on making my dream come true.

But it doesn't. And if you cling to that belief, you *will* become bitter and defeated—a loser in your own mind. Nobody's dream becomes all true. Nobody's.

This Isn't What I Dreamed It Would Be

Those are tough words to hear when you spent much of your life working toward a dream. Maybe you've risked it all, and sunk every ounce of physical and emotional strength you have into your dream. Maybe you've convinced yourself that you're just not trying hard enough—not giving enough—not suffering enough to make your dream come true. Until you embrace the fact that your entire dream will never be reality, you're going to stay in the pain of this crisis, wondering why you're so defeated by life. There's nothing more you can or should do.

Deeply satisfying happiness is about discovering fulfillment in the present moment, not about achieving yesterday's goal. Happiness is about the here and now, not about acquiring what you always wished you had. As long as you live in the past, trying to fulfill wishes you inherited from days now gone, happiness will elude you.

When you were a child, you thought you'd be happy if you had a certain kind of life. A certain kind of husband or wife, a certain kind of job, and a certain kind of family were all in the picture. As the years progressed you became engrossed in your fantasy and tried to make it a reality. What you didn't realize along the way, however, is that while you were busy trying to accomplish the dream, *your dream changed*. The husband you thought you always had to have isn't what you need. Your dream job turned out to be a nightmare. The success you thought you had to have doesn't satisfy you. Your dream changed the closer you got to having it.

So what did you do when the dream changed? The answer to that question is what has brought you to this crisis. You didn't allow the dream to change, and instead clung to yesterday's dream. Now, you're stuck with a dream that is broken and a heart that is crushed.

There's something you need to remember: Dreams are rented and never owned. Dreams are only yours to hold for a period of time, and then you must let them go. If you cling to them, they become like yesterday's manna—they rot in your hands. Dreams are meant to guide your life, not to be your life's destiny. They take you by the hand and lead you along life's path, and when they can no longer be of service to you, you must let them go.

What dream are you unwilling to release?

Is your unrelinquished dream that your son will marry the perfect wife (even though he's been married for years to someone who doesn't fit your dream)? That your career will bring you both great satisfaction and greater wealth? That your marriage will be the ideal romance? That one day your parents will approve of your life?

Many people, particularly around middle age, come to therapy during the painful throes of a crisis about a broken dream. They wake up one day and realize that much of their life isn't what they imagined it would be. Their kids don't appreciate their sacrifices, their spouses aren't as romantic as they could be, or their jobs seem meaningless and unfulfilling. They're overcome with a feeling that they must change something *immediately*. They're in terrible pain and are desperate to regain the dream. Is this you?

If it is, then you're struggling with the "have-it-all" unnatural agreement. This agreement, and the others that follow, are ones you make with yourself and go something like this.

1. I Won't Allow Myself to Be Happy Unless *All* of My Dream Comes True

This agreement is both devastating and cruel, and it only leads to heartache.

Roland would seem to have it all. After a very successful career, starting his own business and growing it into a national corporation, he wants for no material thing. He has more money than he can possibly spend in his lifetime and three houses in the most desirable and exclusive locations on the globe. Yet Roland is chronically discontented.

Why? Because in his mind, he didn't achieve his *entire* dream. He got the part of his dream about achieving professional acclaim and financial gain, but never created the kind of family he wanted. Two divorces and a current unhappy third marriage have broken that dream. Roland is now in his seventies and has resigned himself to being a failure at life. He stays at home much of the time, playing the stock market on his computer.

"Oh!" you say. "If I were Roland, I'd be on top of the world. Nothing could make me unhappy." Well, not necessarily. You see, you are doing the same thing to yourself that Roland is doing. You're forbidding yourself to be happy because you haven't achieved the *whole* dream. "If I only had a better job . . . had a better spouse . . . had more money . . . were thinner . . . had supportive parents . . . had loving children . . . then I could be happy." Just like Roland, you fail to savor the good that has come into your life simply because it isn't *all* good.

You've allowed yourself to destroy your own dream by not allowing the dream to evolve. You dreamed, and some of it came true. The rest wanted to evolve and grow into something better, but you refused to allow it. Instead, you dug in your heels and refused to budge. The child in you screamed, "If I can't have everything I want, then I won't be happy!"

2. My Dreams Are the Only Thing That Will Make Me Happy

Dreams are what you hope will make you happy. When you achieve them, they often do, but not always. Some dreams will make you miserable once you achieve them.

It isn't all that unusual for a businessperson to work his or her whole career to reach the top ranks of a company, and once there, discover that he or she doesn't enjoy the work. Or for a couple to dream of retiring to a farm, and, when they finally do, find they are totally bored and miss the city. Or for an aspiring novelist to wish for the time to write a novel, and when he or she does set aside the time, discover that he or she doesn't really enjoy the process of daily writing and editing.

Your dreams are teachers and guides, helping you to discover more about yourself. Sometimes what they teach you is that you really don't want what you think you might.

On the path to your dream, you may discover something unexpected that pleases you even more than your original dream. Those wonderful opportunities can make you happier than your original dream ever would.

Your dreams are only ideas that you have about what might make you happy. When you reject found happiness simply because it doesn't match your dream, you severely limit your chances of finding much happiness at all.

3. Most Dreams Don't Come True (So What's the Point of Dreaming in the First Place?)

Some dreams come true, and some do not, but without dreams you have no compass for your life. Where are you going? What is it that you want out of life?

This is what a dream gives you: a journey. A dream isn't a destination at all, it is a process for living. When you refuse to dream, you begin to lose your way and your hope in life.

THE TRANCE OF CYNICISM

When you refuse to dream, or when you won't allow your dreams to change and evolve, you sink deep into the trance of cynicism. You have effectively killed your dreams, and now you try to protect yourself from regret by killing everyone else's. You look carefully for the critical flaw in everyone else, the reason why they're deluded or misguided and why their dreams won't come true. It's a twisted trance that you induce, and the price it demands is heavy.

The trance of cynicism has many faces:

◆ A forty-something woman who, after her own marriage failed, chooses to dislike her friends' husbands and is obsessed with their flaws

◆ A mid-career supervisor who assumes everyone who is wealthy got that way dishonestly (because he never became the success he dreamed of becoming)

◆ A mother whose child got into trouble with the law who constantly warns her friends that their children are probably also behaving badly

◆ A young husband who discovered his wife was having an affair with a very wealthy man who now thinks that all women are out to manipulate men to get what they want

◆ A woman who discovered her rabbi was embezzling money who now thinks all religious people are phonies

The trance of cynicism is a surefire recipe for misery. It'll age you beyond your years and twist your heart into a snarled, rigid stone. Because you didn't get your dream (or all of your dream), you inevitably start ridiculing everyone else who is trying to achieve theirs. "It'll never work! You'll end up disappointed! Why try?" you'll tell those around you. Before you know it, you will push away those who love you and find yourself lonely and very unhappy.

The trance of cynicism is born of great pain and sorrow. You didn't get everything you wanted, so you make a lifestyle out of grieving over it. You surround yourself with people who have abandoned their dreams too, so together you can maintain the trance. Life under the trance of cynicism is indeed dreary, but it serves one primary purpose: *It allows you to avoid your own dream.*

You may become bitter, critical, and aloof, but at least you don't have to grapple with your dream, either by paying the cost of following it or by learning how it must be changed.

Is that really the person you want to be? I don't think it is. Part of the art of dreaming is to recognize when to let go of a dream and when to savor a dream realized. You didn't get it all. You never will. But what you have got is precious, if you'll only let yourself see it for what it is.

How is your dream trying to evolve? How are you using the trance of cynicism to keep from facing that fact?

As I write this chapter, my close friend Ron is struggling with a divorce. After thirteen years, the relationship has fallen apart and he is in that difficult place of trying to decide if there is something worth fixing or if it is time for the relationship to end. It's a very tough place that unfortunately many of us know about firsthand.

In the last days before he was to move out of the house, Ron's dog, Tad, died. Tad had been Ron's close companion for many years, as they walked several miles together every morning. On the morning after Tad died, Ron went on his walk alone. Grief-stricken, he walked for hours, passing all the other dog owners he used to see every morning, each one asking about Tad, and having to tell the story over and over again. Ron was overcome with the sense that his whole life was falling apart.

That same morning, I learned that Tad had died and I went out to find Ron. I knew he'd be walking, and sure enough, I found him on his usual trail, walking alone. We stood for a moment and embraced, crying over the loss that was all around him. As we talked, Ron told me an amazing story that I think will speak to you, too.

Earlier that week Ron had begun reading a little book, *The Zen of Oz,* that he found on the sale table at the local bookstore. It was a simple volume that explained the principles of Zen Buddhism through the story of *The Wizard of Oz.* Ron had thoroughly enjoyed the book.

On the trail that morning, something very amazing had happened. He passed an older, vibrant woman who usually fast-walked the same trail in the mornings. As she passed Ron, they greeted each other and moved on. Then, for no reason, she turned back to him and said, "And what about those ruby slippers?" Ron was dumbfounded, since he hadn't told anyone about the book he was reading. Was she referring to the ruby slippers that Dorothy wore on the road to Oz?

Then, as he continued to walk and puzzle over her comment, he turned a corner and there on the side of the trail were two ruby slippers. Well, they weren't exactly ruby, but someone had taken a pair of women's shoes and covered them with sparkling ruby-colored stones. Here in the middle of a walking trail that ran up to Ron's home were two ruby slippers. Can you imagine anything more bizarre?

For Ron the slippers had deep meaning. He was on a journey and passing through a very dark place in life. Dorothy's slippers had protected and guided her all the way to her destiny. Eventually those slippers took her back home to Kansas. The message was clear to Ron. He had a difficult journey ahead, but he had everything he needed to make it to his destination. The ruby slippers reminded him of that all-important fact.

Truthfully, I wasn't sure if Ron had actually seen the slippers or just imagined them through his grief. After we sat on the side of the trail and talked for some time, I walked back up the trail to my car. Wouldn't you know it? There, right where Ron had said they would be, were the pair of ruby slippers. I laughed out loud at how wonderful those homemade slippers were.

Tad's death and the discovery of the ruby slippers is a story about broken dreams. You see, the death of Tad was like the death of an old dream that had walked with Ron for many years. It had guided him through his life and given him many hours of great pleasure. But the day had come to let Tad go, and to move on to another dream. Ron's life was changing and evolving, as it had to. The old dream had died and the new dream was just beginning to bud. The truth of the ruby slippers was that the new dream *would* come and would guide him to his destiny, if he was willing to let it.

Sometimes we all need to be reminded of the ruby slippers on our feet. You have everything you need for happiness and fulfillment. It's when you refuse to keep on the journey toward Oz, and when you refuse to let your dreams grow and guide you, that you fall into trouble. Yesterday's dream was yesterday's guide. The question you must ask is, "What is today's dream?"

Where is your dream taking you, **today?**

The truth that will resolve your crisis of broken dreams is this: "The best dreams always die." Your dreams will never last forever; they all eventually die and new dreams rise up to take their place. Part of the resolution of this crisis is learning to live in the present and to savor today's dreams. They are wonderful guides given to you for a very special purpose. Consume your dreams whole-heartedly and take every bit of inspiration that they can give, knowing that they won't last forever—better yet, knowing that they will eventually be replaced by tomorrow's equally satisfying and exhilarating dreams.

The Four Stages of the Crisis of Broken Dreams

1. Breaking the trance of cynicism

You create a trance of cynicism—believing all dreams to be false—to avoid dealing with the disappointment of your own broken dreams.

2. Confronting the crisis

You acknowledge that, though your whole dream didn't come true, this doesn't mean you don't or won't have a happy and fulfilling life.

3. Sorting through the confusion

You begin to allow old dreams to die and new dreams to be born.

4. Resolving the crisis

You start to dream big dreams and allow those dreams to evolve and change as your life evolves.

THE BREAKTHROUGH JOURNEY:

Get Past Resistance...
and Start Going Somewhere!

Every man dies, but few truly live.
—SIR WILLIAM WALLACE

Now that you have learned how to resolve your crisis, whichever of the seven it might be, there are just a few important things remaining. I'll label all three of them resistance.

GOODBYE, OLD FRIEND!

When you've lived with a crisis at the back door of your life for many years, and now it's gone or is beginning to disappear, it will take some adjusting. There's no burning drama, no threatening feelings beneath the surface waiting to come forth, and no hidden forces driving you. Now, there is an unusual peace.

Feeling that peace and listening to the quiet of your own mind can be disconcerting at first. After all, much of your life to this point has taken its meaning from the crisis you were fighting. Now that you no longer have a battle to fight, what will you do with all that energy? Where will you focus your mind?

You may even be tempted to recreate a crisis to make life more familiar again. You know how to live with unresolved crisis, as painful as it may be, but you may not have experienced life without crisis and that can be a very strange feeling at first. Whether you like it or not, you take comfort in the familiar—even when that "familiar" is a crisis.

The first type of resistance that you'll face is that empty hole left in your life once a crisis is resolved. I know it may sound strange, but this is very real. When you resolve a crisis that has absorbed a great deal of your psychic energy, you're left with time and energy you didn't have before. Sometimes, that can make you very anxious. Anxious enough that some people sabotage their own well-being to avoid dealing with the discomfort.

Living with crisis wasn't a piece of cake, but it was familiar. Once you no longer have to fill your days worrying about a failing relationship or a job you despise, you've got an empty spot in your life you need to fill.

THE DEVIL YOU KNOW IS BETTER THAN THE ONE YOU DON'T

Sometimes, what you don't know seems more frightful than the pain you do know. That's exactly what Jean-Paul Sartre's classic play *No Exit* is all about. It opens with a hotel room in Hell, into which the bellhop introduces three permanent guests, one by one. Each guest is consumed with his or her own desires but is prevented from fulfilling those desires by one of the other guests. Try as they might, not one of the three can find any satisfaction.

When these three guests—so tortuously matched—have brought their unrelenting demands on each other to a fevered pitch of frustration, escape becomes the only possible relief to their suffering. Just then, the locked door of their room swings open, revealing a potential "exit," and the guests, stunned by this change of events, stare into the empty space. Nobody leaves. The door swings shut, and they are locked forever in their chosen cell.

Sartre's depiction of the feared unknown is haunting. Despite the immense suffering of the guests, they preferred their pain to exploring the unknown of the azure void. In their minds, the devil they knew was better than the devil they didn't know.

So it is with a crisis. Sure, a crisis is troubling, but maybe it isn't as troubling as the unknown, untested, new thing you haven't experienced.

The important thing to remember about this fear is that it, like all fears, begins to wane once reality is engaged. In other words, once you allow the time to create a new and different life, you will no longer feel this sense of fear and anxiety.

I remember one client, Julia, who came to see me complaining of depression. It seemed that she had been clinically depressed for years and couldn't seem to shake it.

Along with therapy, I recommended that Julia go on an antidepressant drug to help her overcome the depression. Several weeks after she started the antidepressant medication, her depression began to lift. Ironically, however, another symptom took its place: anxiety. Whereas Julia had been depressed and lethargic before, she was now nervous and worried about life in general.

What Julia experienced is quite common among clients who experience some relief from their painful symptoms only to find that another symptom takes its place. When a crisis so embeds itself in your life, removing it can create a big psychic vacuum. What will I do if I'm not depressed? What will I talk about if I'm not complaining about my husband? What will I think about if I'm not constantly worrying about my children?

You can't let the fear of the unknown steal from you a better life. Pushing through this fear will take away its power to control your destiny. It's a matter of feeling the fear but not acting on it. When you start to feel the uncertainty created by the changes you've made, take immediate action that reminds you of what you want to feel. Watch a movie about someone who is following his or her passion. Take a walk through the park and notice all the people who have joy-filled relationships and remind yourself that you can have this too. Get on your feet by starting to do something positive, no matter how small or insignificant, when you feel yourself slipping back into the old ways. If you think your passion is to become a chef, make sure to try at least one new recipe a month. If your antagonist has kept you from trusting strong men in your life and you are trying to make a change, choose one particular individual you know affects you and make a special effort not to overreact to him. Chart your progress as you go. Reread your list of agreements (from the second chapter) and continue to revise and amend them as they change and develop. Stay aware of the ways in which you are improving and changing your life for the better, whether that means keeping a journal of your journey or discussing it with your confidant. When you do, you'll notice that your fear and anxiety quickly fades and that you are continuing to move toward the life you want to create.

HELP! THEY DON'T WANT ME TO CHANGE

The second form of resistance that you will confront is the reaction of people around you. In short, they may not want you to change. They may actually need the trance you are creating. If you change, they may be forced to confront their own crisis.

Don had for years refused to confront his crisis of passion. Early in his career as an architect he had abandoned his love of design for a more secure job designing warehouses. He thought the money he made from his corporate job would more than compensate for the boring work.

But it never did. Every year that went by, he regretted his career decisions more than before. Finally, in his early fifties, Don announced to his wife, Beth, that he was thinking of leaving his job to join a new architectural firm that would focus on environmentally friendly buildings. It wouldn't pay much, but he expected it to be far more enjoyable.

Beth was horrified. She did everything she could to stop Don from making a career change, even to the point of calling his parents and asking them to intervene. How could he do this to her? How could he switch paths so late in his career?

The truth was, Don and Beth really didn't need the extra money that Don made by working at the corporate job. They had saved well and were financially secure.

What was troubling Beth was something deeper. Early in her career she had abandoned her training as a classical pianist (she had earned a master's degree in piano performance with honors from a well-known music school) to become an executive secretary. She had spent most of her career working for the same executive and earned a very nice living.

After some therapy, it became clear that Beth's anxiety over Don's career was forcing her to face her own suppressed crisis. She had loved the piano and once dreamed of being a concert pianist, traveling the world and playing with symphony orchestras. She had given all this up to help provide for her family.

Don was trying to resolve his crisis, and in doing so, he broke the trance that Beth had created to suppress her own crisis. Beth was being forced by Don's decision to face her own demons.

You have attracted to yourself people who live in the same trance that you do. For example, if no one around you is passionate or has a happy home life, then you don't feel the need for either of these as sharply. When you decide to resolve these crises, the people around you are faced with a dilemma. Your movement toward greater fulfillment only highlights their discontent. They have a vested interest in keeping you from changing.

As you begin to resolve a long-standing crisis, it is important that you surround yourself with others who have also resolved this crisis. You need the support and encouragement for your own process, and you don't need those around you trying to drag you backward.

RUN BY COMMITTEE

The third form of resistance is allowing yourself to be run by the committee of opposing voices in your mind. You know this committee well—the group of bickering voices that keep you from taking action. "Is that really a good idea?" one voice says. "I'm not sure that's the responsible thing to do," another voice chimes in. Before you know it, you're paralyzed. The committee in your mind—as all committees tend to do— holds you hostage with their debate and indecision. As a result, you abandon taking positive action that will resolve your crisis and sink back into a pattern of denial and resistance.

Imagine what a painting would look like if a committee painted it. Or, imagine reading a novel that was written by a committee. Seems ludicrous, right? Well, it is. Committees almost always make decisions that are compromises—and as a result, they take longer and often don't really satisfy the need at hand.

If you want to take positive action in your life, you've got to silence the committee. Once you've confronted your crisis and made the decision to take action toward resolving it, you've got to tune out all the voices that might paralyze you into not taking action. Make the decision, commit to action, and then move on. Sitting around and contemplating all the possibilities won't keep you from making a mistake; it will only keep you from taking positive action.

THE FINAL HURDLE

The path of living without crisis will become familiar and truly joyous in time. First, you've got so much to learn about yourself and life now that you don't have to spend all your time fighting the demons within. In time, you will find great comfort with your new life and wonder how it was that you ever lived such a painful existence.

The key to staying on the path you've chosen is simple: Keep doing the work. Keep examining your life and confronting the questions life poses you, no matter how difficult they may be. *Do something* every day that is focused on supporting yourself in your journey. Start writing in a journal, begin a spiritual practice, see a therapist who supports your growth, join a group of like-minded seekers, spend time with your mentor, read a life-affirming book—the choices you can make toward your own well-being are endless. The real issue at this point isn't the choice itself, it is deciding to make the choice and taking positive action. Regular, positive action is the key to maintaining the gains you've achieved.

Crisis will come into your life again, but now you have the tools to deal with that crisis. You are free to create the life you want to live—not a life that is stuck in the same repeating story. Rather than an unresolved crisis controlling your life, *you* are in control. *You* decide how your life will move forward instead of allowing yourself to be pushed from behind by unresolved crises.

You will feel pain. The difference is, you now know why it is occurring. Knowing why it keeps happening allows you to break the trance and sets you free to resolve the crisis. The crisis is nothing more than a storm that will pass as long as you're willing to go through that storm fully aware and refuse to seek shelter in denial, resistance, and unconscious living.

You've learned that avoiding a crisis is only an illusion. There is no avoiding crisis—to try to avoid it is to find yourself stuck in continual crisis. *The only way out is to go through it.* You'll be challenged by the next crisis, but it doesn't have to defeat you. More important, you don't have to succumb to the crisis's seductive trance. Now you've got the tools to confront your crisis and achieve a breakthrough.

The Eastern religions have long held that every truth is a paradox—a combination of two seemingly contradictory facts. The paradoxical truth about your crisis is that once you face the crisis squarely, no matter how grim it may appear, it will begin to resolve. Only when you refuse to confront your crises do they have the power to hold you back. This is the fundamental truth of this book: *Facing your crisis is the answer to resolving it.*

The choice is yours: Stay locked into the same self-defeating cycle, or free yourself to live life to the fullest. What will you choose?

Notes

WON'T IT EVENTUALLY JUST GO AWAY?

1. Adelaide Bry, *EST: 60 Hours That Transform Your Life* (New York: Harper & Row, 1976), p. ix.
2. Robert M. Alter, *The Transformative Power of Crisis: Our Journey to Psychological Healing and Spiritual Awakening* (New York: HarperCollins, 2000), p. 27.

TRANCES WE LIVE

1. Margaret J. Wheatley, *Leadership and the New Science* (San Francisco: Berrett Koehler Books, 1992), p. 122.

I WANT TO FEEL INSPIRED

1. Gregg Levoy, *Callings: Finding and Following an Authentic Life* (New York: Three Rivers Press, 1997), p. 65.
2. Ibid., p. 68.
3. Don Lee Keith, "Cast in His Own Mold," *Louisiana Cultural Vistas,* Spring 1999, p. 17.
4. Cynthia Kersey, *Unstoppable* (Naperville, Ill.: Sourcebooks, 1998), p. 272.
5. Debbi Fields, *One Smart Cookie* (New York: Simon & Schuster, 1987).

6. "Mrs. Fields Manages Time," *Special Report: Millennial Woman,* CareerPath.com.

7. Sandy Naiman, "Debbi Fields is One Smart Cookie," *Toronto Sun, January 18, 1999.*

8. The American Heritage Dictionary of the English Language, 3d edition (Boston: Houghton Mifflin, 1992), electronic version licensed from InfoSoft International, Inc.

WHO WILL I SHARE MY LIFE WITH?

1. Virginia Satir, *Making Contact* (Berkeley, Calif.: Celestial Arts, 1976) (pages unnumbered).

WHY CAN'T I BELIEVE IN MYSELF?

1. Donald Clifton and Paula Nelson, *Soar with Your Strengths* (New York: Dell Publishing, 1992), p. 44.

2. Holly Brubach, "Doc Rotella's Cure for the Thinking Athlete," *New York Times,* November 2, 1997, p. 46.

HOW CAN I BECOME MY OWN PERSON?

1. Laurie Beth Jones, *The Path* (New York: Hyperion, 1996), p. 35.

I WANT TO BE IN CONTROL OF MY LIFE

1. "Fresh Air," interview with Terry Gross, National Public Radio, 1997.

WHAT DOES IT ALL MEAN?

1. Quoted in Melvin Morse, *Closer to the Light* (New York: Ballantine Books, 1990), p. 112.

2. Viktor E. Frankl, *Man's Search for Ultimate Meaning* (New York: Insight Books, 1997), pp. 17–18.

3.   Ibid., p. 19.

4.   Alice Miller, *Thou Shalt Not Be Aware: Society's Betrayal of the Child* (New York: Penguin Books, 1986), p. 93.